Come Follow Me

Resources for the Period of Inquiry in the RCIA

edited by
Joseph P. Sinwell

PAULIST PRESS

ALSO EDITED BY JOSEPH P. SINWELL WITH KARAN H. POWELL
PUBLISHED BY PAULIST PRESS

Breaking Open the Word of God (Cycle A)
Breaking Open the Word of God (Cycle B)
Breaking Open the Word of God (Cycle C)
(*Resources for Using the Lectionary for Catechesis in the RCIA*)
Ninety Days
(*Resources for Lent and Eastertime in the RCIA*)

Library of Congress Cataloging-in-Publication Data

Come follow me: resources for the period of inquiry in the RCIA/
    edited by Joseph P. Sinwell.
        p. cm.
    ISBN 0-8091-3150-1
    1. Catechumens—Religious life. 2. Christian education of adults—
United States. 3. Catholic Church. Ordo initiationis Christianae
adultorum. 4. Non church-affiliated people—Religious life.
5. Catholic Church—Membership. 6. Conversion. 7. Catholic Church—
Education—United States. I. Sinwell, Joseph P.
BX935.C65 1990
268′.434—dc20
                                                                90-30536
                                                                CIP

Published by Paulist Press
997 Macarthur Boulevard
Mahwah, New Jersey 07430

Printed and bound in the
United States of America

Contents

Dedication

To those whose faith and love first taught
me to follow: Joseph, Beulah, Mark, Gary,
Colleen, Dorothy and Emma;
and those whose faith and love now challenge me
to continue: Elizabeth, Sarah, Benjamin and Luke

Introduction

The period of inquiry in the Rite of Christian Initiation of Adults challenges the Christian community to invite others to seek initiation. This period focuses on the proclamation of the good news and conversion to Jesus Christ. *Come Follow Me* seeks to offer a pastoral tool that will enable those involved in the catechumenate to learn and inquirers to reflect, discuss and pray about the gospel message.

The introductory articles focus on key concerns during the inquiry period. "An Ongoing Precatechumenate Process" provides models and pastoral insights for such inquiry sessions. The other two articles offer pastoral suggestions and reflect on the need for developing spirituality and discernment.

The agenda for inquiry needs to flow from the questions of those who come forth. The sessions identify human issues that often surface from inquirers. The sessions provide a broad array of issues, but are not meant to be lesson plans. Rather, they seek to explore the word of God and motivate towards conversion.

These sessions make the following assumptions:

■ That a parish catechumenate team will be working with inquirers and shaping a catechumenate.
■ That hospitality will be the prime ingredient in each session. Individuals will be warmly welcomed and introduced to each other.
■ That the parish is committed to evangelizing itself.
■ That the agenda for the sessions flows from the inquirers. (These sessions are starting points and do not exhaust possible issues for inquirers.)
■ That the parish catechumenate team promotes principles of adult religious education.
■ That an atmosphere of trust and openness will be created and promoted.

Although this volume is intended for use in the inquiry period, other adults may find this a useful resource for scripture sharing, prayer groups, personal reflection and other adult religious education activities.

I wish to acknowledge the cooperation and creativity of those who have contributed to this book, Mr. Robert Hamma of Paulist Press for his support, and Sharen Wisher for her diligent assistance.

Inviting others to come and join a Christian community is a challenging task. This book is a resource that will enable individuals to come and hear the good news, and to come and follow Jesus.

Marguerite Main

An Ongoing Precatechumenate Process

It is January. The young man is distraught. A much-loved brother is dying of cancer. How can he make sense of this? Where is God in the midst of his pain? Can he come to our church to ask his questions, to inquire? Is there any meaning to be found in this suffering?

It is March. Ann is a young woman, married to a man with mixed feelings about his Catholic "roots." Her coworker recently started attending the Catholic Church again, seeking to find a faith she inherited by baptism but never by practice. Would Ann come with her—"just to see?"

Spring begins to turn into early summer. It is June. Days are longer. Signs of new life are in bloom all around. Someone is working late in the church office. A door is open to let in warm evening breezes. The hesitant young man knocks on the door. Is there anyone there he can talk to about the Catholic faith? He is from a faraway country, well-educated, alone, and searching. Is there some sort of class going on where he could find out about the Catholic faith and ask his life issue questions?

They are a brother and a sister, out for a summer evening walk. Their family life situation is difficult. They sense something lacking. What draws them to the door of the church this hot summer night? What leads them to see the notice in the bulletin posted on the front door: "Can the Catholic Church help you to find meaning in your life? Can God possibly be there for *you?* Come and see . . . every Wednesday night." And they do.

These scenes are not uncommon. They can be found every day in every Catholic parish in the country. The question is: What is there for them in *your* parish when they come knocking, searching . . . in November, in January, in May or July? What signs of welcome or invitation might they find?

It is real people like those mentioned above who first caused our

parish RCIA team to raise questions regarding an ongoing precatechumenate process. We needed to deal with the issue of "readiness"
—*our* readiness to be welcoming and receptive at a time when something in *their* lives created a readiness in them to search, inquire, seek.
We recognized that the nine-month school year model we had been
using was inadequate. A response to any of the above young people
that, "Precatechumenate or inquiry sessions will begin in the fall, and
we will call you at that time" would have been not only a turn-away for
them, but more than likely a door which closed firmly and forever in
their faces. Readiness to seek God's call in one's life cannot be pro-
grammed into a calendar. That is an unfortunate truth for those who
are much more comfortable with neat, efficient scheduling. It means
flexibility, messiness, uncertainty. Who needs it?

We do. The Rite of Christian Initiation of Adults defines the
precatechumenate as "a time, of no fixed duration or structure, for
inquiry and introduction to gospel values, an opportunity for the beginnings of faith." Responding to this raises many questions. Perhaps
the biggest obstacle is *time.* How can I do this? I don't have time for
everything I am doing now. If we begin an ongoing process, we will
have people at many different stages of the process at one time (true!).
How can I handle that?

Let me digress for a moment to mention again the word "team."
The RCIA is *not* another "program" run by the pastor or by the staff
person who has been to a workshop. It is a *parish* responsibility, and
that means that members of the parish participate in the planning,
organizing, catechesis, prayer—in other words, as a parish RCIA
planning team. (For specifics on the selection, formation, and training
of an RCIA team, see *Forming a Catechumenate Team* by Karan
Hinman, Liturgy Training Publications, 1986.)

Questions which the team might address in planning an ongoing
process may include:

- *Who* are the inquirers who come to us?
- How are we reaching out to them?
- What are the life issues which bring them here?
- How can we respond at the moment when they have been
moved to come and raise their questions?

Let me propose two models. The first one has evolved from our
parish experience over the last three years with real life-seekers such as
those mentioned in the first paragraphs. The second model is based on

the concept of small faith-sharing communities, and would be an option in parishes where those communities are a reality.

A Parish Experience

The Invitation:

Come and See. Are you searching for a church to call your own? Do you struggle with questions about life—death—suffering—hope—forgiveness—love—God? Sessions exploring these and other faith issues in relation to our Catholic belief are held *every Wednesday night* 7–9 p.m. in the Parish Center. *Come and See* (or bring someone you know who might be searching).

The first step in beginning an ongoing precatechumenate process is the invitation to those who might be interested in coming, to let them know that they may begin this process at any time. Notices such as the above might be a regular part of the parish bulletin, or perhaps be posted in a conspicuous place on the church bulletin board, be incorporated into a flyer such as "How does one become a Catholic?," or even regularly submitted to the local newspaper. The important thing is to let prospective "inquirers" know that they are welcome at any time.

The Welcome: It is extremely important that a welcoming, non-threatening atmosphere be established for these sessions. It takes a great deal of courage to walk alone into a room full of strangers. Questions for a team to address might be: What can we do to make our environment a welcoming, hospitable sign of who we are? Who is greeting those who arrive, watching out for newcomers hesitantly approaching? What is being done to put them at ease? What impression would a stranger have? What signs are there in the room which "speak our name" as Christian? (Is there a Bible, a cross, a candle? music? banners?) How do we help them feel comfortable in walking through the door the first time? This is a very important first step. It is especially important when it is an ongoing process, and there are others there who already know each other. How do we make that new member feel welcome? How do we tell our names and our stories?

If we have shown ourselves to be a welcoming, searching, inviting community, it is extremely likely that new inquirers will come often, perhaps every week. We may never know who is going to be there. Most who come, once they take that first step, will come regularly if we have done our job well; but since it is ongoing, people do have the freedom to drop out for a time if necessary, with the knowledge that we will still be there to welcome them back when they return. While we tell them they are free to come and go, we also emphasize that their discernment about future commitment to baptism or full communion will be helped by regular participation.

The Agenda: Amazing things have happened since our structure for inquiry has changed. We switched our focus from imparting doctrine neatly wrapped in a slick book, to helping the inquirer focus on the mystery of God's presence within his or her own experience. This focus was always there; however, in the past, dialogue, questions, and sharing had been scheduled according to *our* agenda.

Now we let the inquirers set the agenda from week to week, As each week's session ends, we ask them to set the agenda for the following week. This sets a more leisurely pace as we realize we can spend as much time as necessary with any one issue. When it is *their* agenda, not ours, the questions raised are relevant and meaningful to the inquirers, while the depth of their sharing is overwhelming to us.

Our sessions are flexible, but there is a definite purpose. The leaders come prepared to share a particular aspect of the good news. Based on this, we share where we've been and where we are going in light of God's word and our Catholic tradition. We share what we believe within the context of who we are. As we participate in what has become a mutual learning experience, we come to recognize each inquirer for what he or she is: a true treasure, God's gift to us.

Newcomers to the group are ministered to by those who have been attending longer. As we tell and retell our own stories, the depth of sharing increases, and new meanings are seen in retold stories. In addition, experiences brought to the group by newcomers open up completely different lines of thought for us to pursue.

An Alternative Model

For those parishes where ongoing small faith communities are a reality, I present an alternative model for the ongoing catechumenate. The Introduction to the Rite of Christian Initiation of Adults states "The initiation of catechumens is a gradual process that takes place within the community of the faithful" (#4). If small faith-sharing communities are meeting regularly, how better to incorporate the inquirer into the community of the faithful than to open these small groups to welcome an inquirer into them. If these groups meet monthly, or twice a month, an inquirer would be invited to meet regularly with them. This would have the advantage of having them experience first-hand the faith of the Catholic community, and might also have the added benefit of providing a sponsor or sponsors from that small group when the inquirer is ready to become a catechumen.

If such a process were used, it would be important also for these inquirers to meet together as a group during the remaining two or three weeks of the month. Bonding is an essential ingredient in the catechumenate process, and it is equally important for them to form a community among themselves as well as with the larger community. It is in these "inquirers only" sessions that they may feel more comfortable in raising some of the issues and questions they have about their life issues. The opportunity, however, to let an inquirer also be a part of an existing faith community might have long-lasting effects in helping the neophyte later feel more a part of the total parish community.

Discernment

At what point does an inquirer become a catechumen? With an ongoing precatechumenate process, this will obviously not be something that you can automatically schedule ahead on the calendar. We have found that two to three times a year we might have inquirers ready to take this step. The timing depends on them, not on us. If the process is explained to them when they come for a preliminary interview or to the first session, and if they are regularly given opportunities to talk one-on-one with team members, it will become obvious when they are ready to make this decision. Some of the questions which may help them to discern their readiness might include:

■ Am I helped to find God here in this community?
■ Am I becoming comfortable in worshiping here?
■ Am I beginning to see that following Jesus may cause me to make some changes in my life?
■ Am I able to accept that I am loved unconditionally by God?

The length of time that a person might remain in the precatechumenate has varied in our parish from six weeks to more than a year. Much depends on the person's background and previous acquaintance with Catholicism or another Christian religion. Since the rite recommends that the catechumenate period itself (the second period) should last for a minimum of one year, there should be no hurry to try to move inquirers along quickly in order that they may make a particular deadline. The rite states that "after hearing the mystery of Christ proclaimed, (adults) consciously and freely seek the living God and enter the way of faith and conversion as the Holy Spirit opens their hearts" (#1). It is the Holy Spirit who dictates the calendar, not us!

Messy? Yes. Challenging? Yes. Neat and orderly? No. But then, neither is life neat and orderly. If an ongoing precatechumenate is begun, it should be obvious that it would then lead to an ongoing catechumenate. This means that at any given time of the year, you may have inquirers, catechumens, (and during Lent, elect), and neophytes. This will take the time, energy, and resources of a large number of people. Yet it helps to ensure that "initiation takes place within the community of the faithful" where it belongs, as more and more members of the community are invited to be present as sponsors, facilitators, catechists, welcomers, etc. The hospitality and welcoming of those members of the community who participate contribute to the sense of trust and belonging which assists the inquirer in feeling comfortable within the community.

What have been the advantages of this? We have felt that we have been truly ready and welcoming for people when they have felt moved to come "seeking." By letting them set the agenda instead of using a book or setting the agenda ourselves, we feel that we have more faithfully met them where they were, and addressed the issues that were of concern to them. By removing the pressure of following the "school year" calendar, we have been able to feel more comfortable with the readiness of the individual candidates as they move at their own pace to the next period of the process. The extended length of the overall process has given more time for the integration into the parish community, and has in general created a greater sense of belonging, both to the parish as a whole and to the RCIA community. There has been more time and more opportunity for them to both individually and as a group participate in the life of the parish, including a willingness to respond to the gospel message through acts of service.

What are the problems? It requires a team; it is not a "one-man show." The first step for a parish considering an ongoing process should be to begin to recruit and develop a team. It is also uncertain. What if no one comes some evening when you have scheduled the ongoing precatechumenate? That's all right. I don't know anyone who would mind an unexpected free night. Or what if only one person shows up? Some of our most rewarding evenings have been when we have only had one or two, and the sharing has been intense.

The RCIA is primarily about conversion. It is not just about learning doctrines from catechisms. It is enabling people to experience a deeper and deeper relationship with God through reflecting on and being challenged by the message of the gospel. It is about transformation, not information; about relationship, not dogma. Although the passing on of our traditions and teachings is important, we are called beyond that to reflect on the Christian experience and how we individually and collectively respond to those teachings and to the gospel. This type of conversion cannot be hurried or programed. We must be ready to meet someone with open hands and hearts when the Holy Spirit moves them to "come and see." Only in this way can we truly be a welcoming faith community.

Ron Lewinski

The Inquiry Period:
Issues and Pastoral Suggestions

The period of evangelization and precatechumenate, also referred to as the inquiry period, sets the tone for the full process of formation and initiation of Christians. This is the time when the inquirer first meets the community. This is the period when inquirers express their desire to know more about the Catholic Church, questioning perhaps some of the facts and stories they have heard about the church. Some inquirers approach the local parish already determined to accept the Catholic Church as their own. Others come with a very uncertain attitude, openly searching and wondering whether this church will meet their expectations and satisfy their needs. The way in which these inquirers are received will set the stage for what will follow in the months or years ahead. If a good foundation is laid during this period, the catechumenal process will effectively build upon the relationships and basic principles of faith and church established in this first period.

Who Are the Inquirers?

Parishes implementing the RCIA may encounter inquirers from a wide range of backgrounds. There are inquirers who are *unbaptized and uncatechized.* They may have very little religious formation or exposure to religious institutions in their background. They seem to fit the ideal picture of inquirers that the RCIA presents in its model structure.

There are many inquirers who, although they are unbaptized, nevertheless already have a deep faith in God and may by experience or association with others know and appreciate what the church and the Christian life are all about.

The most common inquirers are *baptized but uncatechized Christians.* A typical profile is someone who was baptized as an infant but received very little formal religious formation. Some may have participated in a catechetical or Bible program as a child but ordinarily never became an active church member as an adult. Although they are already membered to Christ and his church by virtue of this baptism, baptized uncatechized persons ordinarily approach the parish with the same feelings and questions and at a level of personal spiritual development similar to unbaptized people.

The above group may also include *baptized but uncatechized Catholics* desiring to complete their initiation through the sacraments of confirmation and eucharist. Baptized but uncatechized Catholics need to be distinguished clearly from returning Catholics who may have been inactive in the church for a number of years. Returning Catholics will ordinarily need a process of healing, reconciliation and reintegration into the church. The questions, issues and experience of returning Catholics will be quite different from the unbaptized or baptized but uncatechized adult. It is best to minister to the returning Catholic through a separate model of formation.

The parish may also encounter *baptized and catechized Christians* who seek to join the Roman Catholic community. These are men and women originally baptized in a Christian denomination who have received a firm foundation in the Christian tradition and may have been an active member of their church. Now, for any number of reasons, they may wish to enter into full communion with the Roman Catholic Church. Ordinarily this group of individuals do not need to participate in the full RCIA process, including the inquiry period. After assessing their needs through pastoral interview, those components of the RCIA process that may be helpful can be applied to them.

Children of catechetical age may also be among the inquirers at parish encounters. The children may be brought to the parish at their parents' initiative. Other children may come on their own seeking the sacrament of initiation. The issue of children and the catechumenate deserves special pastoral attention which this book is not able to provide because of length. However, many of the principles and pastoral ideas found here could be applied to children.

Personal Interview

Before a pastoral team can appropriately minister to inquirers they need to conduct a thorough personal interview with each inquirer. One purpose of the interview is to determine whether the inquirer is baptized or unbaptized and what religious affiliation his or her background might include. The important purpose, however, is to initiate an open and friendly relationship that will allow for an honest dialogue about the inquirer's questions, issues, and personal history.

The interview may be conducted by any member of the pastoral staff or catechumenate team who has good listening skills and is able to help the inquirer feel comfortable, unthreatened, and genuinely heard and respected.

The one who interviews will want to catch a sense of the inquirers' personality and spiritual development. Are they familiar with the Catholic Church? Do they read the Bible? Do they have any regular practice of prayer? What do they value? What are they looking for? What is it at this point in their lives that brings them to the church? Are there Catholics who have influenced their quest?

All of the above questions do not constitute a check list, let alone an exhaustive list of issues that might be discussed. It simply opens a range of possible questions into a person's life that in turn can help us better understand who the inquirer is and what he or she needs. The term "interview" may imply something too formal. It is intended to be neither an application test nor a diagnostic psycho-spiritual evalua-tion. It may take a few encounters—some of them over coffee or at a barbecue—before the pastoral ministers have a clear enough picture of who the inquirers are, before the team can appropriately minister to them.

It is conceivable, of course, in the process of the initial interviews that one may assess that a particular individual is not really looking for what the catechumenate and initiation can promise. Occasionally one might also discern that a potential inquirer is really in need of coun-seling or more serious professional help. Although these judgements have to be made carefully, the possibility for a referral to the appro-priate professionals has to be taken seriously.

In any case, it is only after the catechumenate team has a collec-tive profile of the inquirers that they can begin to plan the precatechu-menate sessions. The design, dynamic and personal approach the team will use in the precatechumenate will be greatly influenced by their appreciation of who the participants are.

Marriage Issues

One of the most painful experiences in catechumenate ministry is encountering difficult canonical marriage issues. An individual has a spiritual reawakening. He or she approaches the Catholic Church with a sincere desire to answer what he or she feels is God's call to a deeper spiritual life. Then we discover that the person is in a second marriage and will need a declaration of nullity or an annulment before the individual can celebrate the sacraments of initiation. Suddenly there is an obstacle to the inquirer's movement toward complete initiation. What do we do?

First of all, the marital status of the inquirer needs to be surfaced as early as possible, probably during the first interview. Pastoral ministers may feel uncomfortable raising canonical marriage issues with inquirers who have no idea that their marital history has any bearing on their desire to join the church. Inquirers' reactions range from confusion and anger to resigned disappointment and humble willingness to do whatever is necessary to become a Catholic.

Effectively handling canonical marriage issues demands some education on the part of the pastoral ministers. The canonical issues surrounding a previous marriage which the church still recognizes as valid and binding are complex and cannot be adequately treated here. The catechumenate team needs to work closely with the diocesan chancery and marriage tribunal in properly handling these pastoral issues.

From a positive standpoint, catechumenate ministers need to understand that what underlies church law regarding marriage is the firm belief in the dignity and permanence of the marriage bond. While it is painful and frustrating to meet the obstacle of applying for an annulment before initiation can occur, it reinforces the basic teaching of the church in regard to the sacredness and permanence of Christian marriage.

It would be unfair and unjust to the inquirer to ignore the church's discipline in this regard simply because the pastoral minister does not feel it is important or appropriate. The inquirer has the right to know exactly where the church stands on the marriage issue. In accepting the church, inquirers need to accept the church as it is and not simply as one particular minister would want to present it.

Furthermore, one should not presume that dealing with a previous marriage cannot in fact be an occasion for healing old wounds through sensitive pastoral care. Handled properly, the process of an annulment can be a very revealing and spiritually fruitful time.

In those cases where a formal canonical process is not able to remove the impediments to a valid marriage, the pastoral staff needs to consult with the local marriage tribunal for appropriate pastoral action.

Should the inquirer be accepted into the precatechumenate before the canonical marriage issues are resolved? Inquirers may be accepted into the precatechumenate as long as they clearly understand that they will not be able to proceed beyond the catechumenate period before the marriage issue is resolved. The reason for this is that a person who is in a canonically irregular marriage is not free to celebrate the sacraments. Therefore it would be inappropriate to receive someone into the church but then require that the individual not receive the sacraments.

Some catechumenate ministers have come to the conclusion that it is better not to receive the inquirers into the RCIA process until the marriage situation is resolved. They reason that once the inquirers become part of a group, it is difficult to hold them back when it is time to celebrate the Rite of Election and the sacraments of initiation. Even when the inquirers have been warned early in the process that they will not be received into the church at the current year's Easter Vigil, there is inevitably a terrible feeling of disappointment, and sometimes of resentment and anger. Pastoral teams need to consider the matter carefully and adopt a policy they can live with. If inquirers are not taken into the process immediately, they still are entitled to the parish's pastoral care.

What Are We Trying To Do During This Period?

One of the ways to get a sense of what needs to happen during the inquiry period is to reflect on what the RCIA states is necessary before the rite of Acceptance Into the Order of Catechumens is celebrated:

> #42. The prerequisite for making this first step is that the beginnings of the spiritual life and the fundamentals of Christian teaching have taken root in the candidates. Thus there must be evidence of the first faith that was conceived during the period of evangelization and precatechumenate and of an initial conversion and intention to change their lives and to enter into a relationship with God in Christ. Consequently, there must also be evidence of the first stirrings of repentance, a start to the practice of calling upon God in prayer, a sense of the Church, and some experience of the company and spirit of Christians through contact with a priest or with members of the community. The candidates should also be instructed about the celebration of the liturgical rite of acceptance.

The heart of the above description reminds us that what the precatechumenate needs to foster is the first evidence of faith, an initial conversion, intention to change one's life, and to enter into a relationship with God in Christ. All of this is supported and encouraged by the community's active engagement with the inquirers.

The expectation in the above paragraph (#42) is very basic and is best understood alongside of #36, which states about the period of precatechumenate: "It is a time of evangelization: faithfully and constantly the living God is proclaimed and Jesus Christ whom he has sent for the salvation of all." Evangelization is the seed that leads to initial faith and conversion.

Evangelization, faith and conversion sound so basic that we are likely to think that we may not need a period of inquiry if most of our inquirers already believe in God and give evidence of a living faith. However, the issue of evangelization runs much deeper than what may appear on the surface. We need to hear about the inquirer's image of God. Has his or her relationship to God changed since childhood? Does the inquirer believe in the goodness of God or have personal misfortune or the tragic events in the news left doubts behind? Is the person of Jesus real to the inquirer or just a religious figure from the past? How does the message of the cross impinge upon the inquirer's life?

The work of the precatechmenate period is to introduce inquirers to the living God and the risen Christ in our midst. Christian belief does not rest on an intellectual adherence to abstract religious truths but upon a mature relationship with the Lord.

Evangelization means more than just fostering a general belief in God. Evangelization is the presentation of the gospel in such a way that the teaching of Jesus becomes an invitation to a new way of life.

The process of evangelization is accomplished in the real world. The gospel is proclaimed in the midst of a world that is often at odds with the way of Jesus. The heart of Jesus' teaching, the reign of God, rubs up against whatever society may value at the time. Were Jesus' mandate for justice, peace, simplicity of heart, love and truth intended to be lived out in some imaginary isolated religious sphere, the process of conversion would be much more easily achieved. But to live by the standards of God's reign in the midst of the real world immediately creates a tension and a challenge for the believer.

To love and admire the Jesus who cures the blind man, raises Lazarus from the dead, turns water into wine and multiplies loaves and fishes is easy compared to believing in what Jesus stands for. Take up the cross. Leave all behind. Forgive seventy times seven. Love your enemies. Pray for those who persecute you. Imitate the little children. Be compassionate as your heavenly Father is compassionate. Be the servant of all. Do not worry about what you are to eat and wear. Do not judge others. All these expectations of the reign of God are hard to own yet essential for one who would accept the call to discipleship. And even these dicta may sound innocent enough until we open our eyes to the real world of our personal lives and the society that envelops us. This is the foundation for a growing sensitivity for social justice and responsibility for our brothers and sisters.

While many of the inquirers may have reached this point in their religious development, the call to believe in the reign of God with all its implications is often still to be heard.

Where Do We Begin?

How does a pastoral team approach the precatechumenate period? Where do we begin? The answer quite simply is with the life stories of the inquirers. We believe that God is revealed in the experiences of their lives. When inquirers approach us we can be sure that God is already at work in their lives. Catechumenate ministers do not give God to inquirers but help them to see and recognize the presence of God in their lives.

The life experiences of the inquirers then is read alongside of the word of God which throws new light into human stories. The word of God challenges us to look at our lives from the critical perspective of the reign of God. God's word stretches our minds and hearts to move beyond where we may presently be to where God may be calling us.

What the Precatechumenate Is Not

Perhaps it would be helpful to say what the precatechumenate *is not*. It is not a time for heavy doctrinal teaching. It does not begin with abstract creedal statements that we discuss as we might in a theology class. It is not the time for an unchanging syllabus designed by the team prior to meeting the candidates. It always begins with the life experiences of the inquirers. It consists of the questions, issues, doubts, fears and convictions that emerge from the experience of the inquirers. Because they will be expected to live their faith in the real world, we welcome the world of their experience and strive to lead them to an initial conversion, to the first stirrings of repentance, to calling upon God in prayer, to a sense of the living church (see RCIA #42). The forty sample sessions in this book offer an example of what those precatechumenate gatherings might look like.

No doubt there will also be the typical "Catholic" questions that emerge. What is holy water? Is the pope really infallible? Why do Catholics pray to Mary? These are reasonable questions that inquirers raise from their association with Catholics or from hearsay. It is all part of the Catholic picture. It is appropriate to answer the questions simply when they arise. It is not necessary in the precatechumenate to give the entire history and theological meaning and significance to every question inquirers raise. A brief answer now can suffice until a more thorough catechesis is offered during the catechumenate period.

Basic Attitudes

Above all, during the precatechumenate period, a spirit of trust and openness needs to be fostered. By keeping company with Catholics through the inquiry period inquirers can begin to naturally catch the spirit of Catholicism. As the trust begins to build the potential becomes greater for a deeper sharing of the experiences of life in dialogue with the word of God.

Prayer has a place in the precatechumenate period, although there is a need to be sensitive to those who have not yet come to believe and have not yet made prayer a part of their lives. The catechumenate team can plan to use very simple forms of prayer and by praying "in spirit and truth" themselves, model the prayer of Catholic Christians to inquirers.

The most effective precatechumenate is found in a parish that is alive with the spirit of the gospel. It is unreasonable to expect a catechumenate team to pass on the values of the reign as our hearts' treasure, if the inquirers cannot catch any glimpse of the reign in the parish.

One way to approach the matter is to ask, "What does our parish stand for?" "Are the beliefs and values of the parish bold enough to be seen and felt by the larger community?" The task of evangelization cannot be left in the hands of a few nor reduced to a program. Evangelization needs to be a charism of the parish that surrounds and incites inquirers and those who have not yet even taken that step. This is what it means when the RCIA states that "the initiation of adults is the responsibility of all the baptized" (RCIA #9).

Barbara Zanin

Discernment in
the Inquiry Period

To discern is to perceive, to discriminate. Christian discernment is a process activity wherein an individual enters into a close examination of his/her historical and experiential self in dialogue with the word of God (especially the gospels), so as to discover God's call. Those who aspire to Roman Catholicism look at the long tradition of other faith-filled persons in history. The activity of discernment is not done in isolation from others, but rather is shaped and challenged by other persons of faith. It is that search for the deepest meaning of one's life centered in the person of Jesus of Nazareth. One who discerns, identifies and decides in his/her personal life what needs to grow and what needs to be let go of in order to follow Christ Jesus. The process of discernment leads to a conscious, but timely decision to follow and participate in the mystery of Jesus' life, suffering, death, and resurrection as that mystery unfolds in the midst of a community of faith. For one who is journeying in the Rite of Christian Initiation of Adults (RCIA), discernment is essential, otherwise there is no measurement which reliably points to the occurence of conversion. Discernment in the RCIA takes all of the above into consideration as the individual and the community determine the appropriate timing for a person to move from one period to another. The period of inquiry/precatechumenate is flavored by a genuine environment of freedom and hospitality within which those who inquire can begin their quest for God in the Roman Catholic tradition. Questions are asked, faith stories are told, the good news of Jesus is proclaimed. In this context, discernment takes place.

The Rite of Christian Initiation of Adults guides the discernment process by providing specific prerequisites to be met before an individual moves from the period of inquiry/precatechumenate to the period of the catechumenate, RCIA (#42). The beginnings of the spiritual life and the fundamentals of Christian teaching have taken root in the

candidates. Thus, there must be evidence of first faith that was con-
ceived during the period of evangelization and precatechumenate, of
initial conversion and intention to change their lives and enter into a
relationship with God in Christ. Consequently, there must also be
evidence of the first stirrings of repentance, a start of the practice of
calling upon God in prayer, a sense of the church, and some experience
of the company and spirit of Christians through contact with a priest or
other members of the community RCIA (#18). The Rite of Acceptance and Welcome should not be too early, but should be delayed
until the candidates, according to their own dispositions and situation,
have had sufficient time to conceive an initial faith and to show the
first signs of conversion.

Polarities of Conversion

Father Robert Duggan, in a talk on spirituality, speaks about
three polarities of conversion which I think are very helpful to those
who seek to know that the issues of discernment the Rite speaks of are
being dealt with in a general way. Father Duggan says, "Conversion is
a work of grace which goes beyond what any one of us can do for
ourselves but at the same time conversion requires, demands a human
response. Conversion involves turning points in the lives of people:
privileged times which crystalize a specific situation and at the same
time continue an ongoing process, a life project. The context of conversion is the uniquely intimate, personal encounter between an individual and God's love, and at the same time while uniquely intimate,
conversion is totally public, an ecclesial event.

Employing these polarities of conversion at the service of discernment during the period of inquiry could help the community and
inquirers be aware of change/conversion as it is occurring. Indeed, the
role of the community during inquiry is to challenge itself and the
inquirer to focus upon the many ordinary ways in which God graces
and invites in freedom an individual to know of God's initiative and to
foster the storytelling of these graced moments. Also, the community's
role in the discernment process is to help persons make appropriate
responses to this loving God. Many adults have never named their
experience of God though everyone has experienced God. Unless the
naming happens it is unlikely that an authentic and conscious decision
to respond will happen.

Each inquirer, encouraged by others, is called to pay special attention to this turning point in his/her own life; to come to grips with

the real issues and questions of life and faith, right here, right now as well as to see that turning to the Lord with one's life is a life project. Paying special attention to this particular life situation includes a scrutiny of all the relationships and events of this moment while at the same time recognizes that with new eyes and a new open heart one will be affected by God's presence for a lifetime.

The community needs to pay careful attention with the person to the unique way God is present to each one and draw them to conclude that in isolation no one comes to know the Lord. During this period of inquiry it is key that persons come to know and to value the community of faith which is church. To be a Roman Catholic is to see oneself as one of many members of the Body of Christ; to see one's natural gifts discovered, nurtured and used for the sake of others. Therefore, during the inquiry period, this movement from isolation to community is an essential activity.

Discernment of Readiness for the Catechumenate

An application of Thomas Goome's praxis movements to the particular issues of discernment which are spelled out in the Rite could be a vehicle for helping one discern and decide readiness to move from the period of inquiry to the catechumenate period. Groome's praxis is comprised of the following movements:

1. Name the present action story
2. Critically reflect
3. Listen to the Christian story and vision
4. Unite the story to my story
5. Respond to vision with vision

The particular issues which are the basis for discernment are grouped in the following ways:

1. Beginnings of the spiritual life
   Enter into a relationship of God in Christ
   Practice of calling upon God in prayer
2. Intention to change their lives
   First stirrings of repentance
3. A sense of the church
4. Fundamentals of Christian teaching

Let us place into conversation these focuses for discernment and Groome's five movements. The use of these movements will serve as a reflective measuring tool for decision regarding movement from inquiry to the catechumenate. Two issues will be dealt with in detail.

1. Beginnings of the Spiritual Life

According to Richard McBrien, to be spiritual in a Christian sense is "the cultivation of a style of life consistent with the presence of the Spirit of Christ within us and with our status as members of the Body of Christ. Christian spirituality has to do with our way of being Christian in response to the call of God, issued through Jesus Christ in the power of the Holy Spirit."[1] The Rite says clearly that there should be the beginnings of the spiritual life, prayer with God and relationship with Christ. A first step for the faith community to take with inquirers is to help them identify the ways they have come to know of God in their daily living: in relationships, in prayer, (Groome 1), and to test the waters by asking what has influenced my prayer and my awareness of God's presence. The community can help them and their sponsors to critically reflect upon what has shaped their past and current experience of God and prayer (Groome 2). The community can examine a variety of ways in which individuals and the community listen for the "tiny voice of God" (in nature, in relationships, in formal and liturgical prayer, scriptural, meditative and contemplative prayer and ask how people throughout our tradition have come to notice and respond to God's presence in their lives. Inquirers also need to begin to experience the richness of God's presence in the scriptures as a life source in prayer (Groome 3). Throughout the precatechumenate period, each inquirer would be challenged to examine the new ways in which his/her spiritual life, a way of being Christian, has deepened (Groome 4). In terms of spirituality and discernment, the faith community would ask: How have you noticed growth in the manner, frequency and depth of your relationship in prayer with God and with others? Are you ready to move into the period of the catechumenate with an openness that will deepen this way of living? How has this experience of prayer, communally and individually readied you to take a next step (Groome 5)?

2. Intention to Change Their Lives

Throughout the inquiry period, the community of faith through catechesis and sponsorship helps people to name the reality of their lives. In the musical *Music Man* the salesman says "you gotta know the territory." Knowing the territory of our lives is the foundation which supports discernment. To uncover/discover/explore the foundation is to identify how each person currently names the activity of daily living; in our families, work and job contexts. The best action we can do as a faith community is model our own struggles to know and name our own reality (Groome 1). We can ask people to respond to the questions: Why do I do what I do? What are the influences which impinge on me to shape my day-to-day attitudes and behaviors? What negative cultural influences invite my involvement, such as materialism, individualism, militarism, competitiveness, etc.? (Groome 2). Those who surround the inquirers through personal witness and sharing of the good news of the gospel and our tradition would present the story based primarily on the gospels (Groome 3). James Digiacomo once said, "Whenever there is authentic preaching of the gospel there is resistance." This movement of Groome's enables persons to note those resistances to change in light of the story, the gospel. Through gospel dialogue, persons will be empowered to understand that to live the Christian life is to live a life of repentance of that which is sinful in each of our lives, and to change that into a life filled with love and charity modelled on Jesus (Groome 4). And finally, a response question follows: *What does it mean for each inquirer to begin to live into a vision of transformation of attitude and behavior which is the beginning of the intention to change life (Groome 5)?*

Discernment Questions

This article has discussed two of the four issues for discernment as prescribed by the Rite in conversation with Thomas Groome's praxis movements. The other two could be developed by the reader in the same manner. The following questions are offered to assist the community and the inquirers to discern readiness in each of the four areas.

Beginnings of the Spiritual Life

What is your current experience of noticing and acknowledging the presence of the Lord in your daily life? How do you pray?

How is God present to you in nature, alone, with others, at worship? How do you praise, petition and thank God in your daily life?

Ask the person to articulate how he/she has grown in an appreciation and habit of prayer both communal and personal, during this journey of inquiry.

Fundamentals of Christian Teaching

The agenda of inquiry is on the questions and stories of faith of the inquirer. Did the inquirers feel free to ask the questions of faith and life that were in their hearts? Were we responsible in our response to those questions? Do the inquirers have a solid grasp of the heart of the Christian message?

A Sense of the Church

Have the inquirers been exposed to the pluralism, unity and vitality of the sign of Jesus in the world? This means that not only do inquirers receive hospitality from parishioners, but also gain a sense of the church universal. Have they gained a sense of the justice and peace message which is the thrust of the church's apostolic mission? Do they have a sense that Christ came for all people and that the Roman Catholic way is a particular and peculiar way in which Christians live out the mystery of Jesus? Has each inquirer gained a feeling of belonging to a faith community as well as a sense of growing identity with that community?

Intention to Change Their Lives

Has the inquirer been empowered to name the real sense of her life in freedom and trust? Has the inquirer recognized many of the graced parts of life as well as some specific areas of growth? Has this person begun to respond to the Lord in her own life and does she see the beginnings of this change in a concrete manner?

If the inquirer can make a positive assent to most of the questions and issues raised in this article, it would seem that a decision to celebrate the Rite of Acceptance/Welcome is correct. If there are major gaps then an extension of time and attention in the period of precatechumenate would be necessary.

It is important for those in leadership in the parish RCIA to realize that their role is not that of judgment regarding readiness for movement from the period of inquiry to the catechumenate. Rather, their role is to empower, unleash, unpack with the inquirers each of the issues/questions of discernment as outlined in the Rite in order that the inquirer make the decision as to when God calls each person to a deeper realm of conversion. Ultimately, questions of Christian discernment rest with a person and a loving God in the context of a Christian community.

NOTE

1. Richard McBrien, *Catholicism* (Minneapolis; Winston Press Inc., 1981) pp. 1057–58.

Joseph P. Sinwell

General Introduction to All Inquiry Sessions

Kim has been working in a young, growing computer business. Her childhood religion had been Shintoism. Many of her friends are Catholic. Because of them, and other circumstances, she is interested in finding out more about the Catholic faith. Ben, born of Christian parents was never baptized. Recently he has experienced rough times. He is asking questions about Jesus and faith. These two persons are seekers. They are inquirers because they desire to discover who is God, who are Christians, and what are implications of becoming a Catholic. The parish can welcome and invite these two persons into a precatechumenate.

The purpose of the precatechumenate period is to evangelize toward conversion to Jesus Christ: it is a time of introduction to gospel values. The Rite of Christian Initiation of Adults states, "The whole period of the precatechumenate is set aside for this evangelization, so that genuine will to follow Christ and seek baptism may mature" (#37). This period of evangelization promotes hospitality and acceptance, and involves listening, storytelling, praying and searching.

In precatechumenate or inquiry sessions, catechists need to listen to those who are inquirers. They can enable inquirers to share their own stories of faith and be open to discovering a living God and the vital church. These sessions focus on common life topics and issues. By touching the experience of the inquirers catechists can bring alive the gospel reality.

To begin with the experiences of the inquirers differs from starting with an explanation of the dogmas of faith. Experience can lead to exploring how the gospel relates to human life. Through the testimony and faith of the catechists and the community, inquirers will find Christ in the ordinary events of their lives. Sessions are to be based on the questions and needs of the inquirers. These sessions reflect common experiences and concerns of inquirers. They are meant only as starting points and practical examples of inquiry sessions.

Another purpose of the precatechumenate period is to motivate the individual to develop a personal relationship with Jesus. One of the ways a person comes to know Jesus and Catholicism is through the gospel stories, personal stories of Christian witness or community stories. Storytelling enlightens the gospel message and emphasizes a personal and communal dimension to believing in Jesus Christ.

A wise person once said the key to praying is to pray. Sessions should include the variety of prayer forms in Roman Catholic tradition. These ways of praying will promote a dialogue and meditation with Jesus Christ. Through prayer individuals may grow in deeper realization of the gospel through the prompting of the Holy Spirit and be disposed to journey toward conversion in Christ Jesus.

Conversion is a key goal of the inquiry period. How does the catechumenate team and parish community promote change? The community needs to witness in attitudes and behavior the gospel values of healing, acceptance, and compassion. Kim and Ben have some questions; their attitude of questioning or searching needs to be fostered. Catechists can create dynamic ways of helping inquirers to continue to search. The sessions will articulate reflections, questions and discussions that can lead to examining one's faith life. Conversion aims at: "How will my belief in Jesus Christ and a vibrant Roman Catholic Church make a difference in my life." The inquiry period focuses on the person's willingness to believe in Jesus Christ and seek initiation into the Roman Catholic community.

The inquiry period provides an excellent opportunity to reach out and welcome those who seek catechumenate. The challenge is to discover creative ways to enable individuals like Kim and Ben to grow in a relationship to the dynamic person of Jesus Christ as revealed in the scriptures, and to encourage, support and stimulate conversion to a gospel way of life by providing ways of listening, storytelling, praying and searching. These sessions will hopefully enable inquirers and catechists to hear, experience and live the Word made flesh.

Joseph P. Sinwell

Introduction to Inquiry Sessions

The period of inquiry focuses on the proclamation of the good news in Jesus Christ and encourages inquirers to come and follow Jesus. These sessions begin with human experiences and try to enable the word of God to penetrate experience and motivate conversion. The sessions are meant as starting points. The outlines need to be adjusted to the specific group. Whenever a catechist is asked to offer a story or experience, as an alternative an appropriate person from the community could be invited to respond to the request. Journal keeping would be helpful for reflection. A general outline of the sessions follows.

Topic identified will be from human experience.

Exploring Experience. This section will try to identify experiences of the inquirers relevant to the topic. Participants will be encouraged to reflect and dialogue about these experiences.

Exploring the Word of God. This section will proclaim parts of the word of God that are pertinent to the topic and elicit a response in discussion or reflection. Leaders need choose the readings or activities appropriate to the group.

Praying. This section will engage the inquirers in different prayer forms in Roman Catholic tradition related to the topic.

Gospel Challenge. This section will present ways of living the message of God's word, thus encouraging conversion. This effort will require reflection in and after session.

RESPONSIBILITY

Responsibility means accountability for one's actions. It also means the ability to respond. Each mature adult has a variety of responsibilites: work, family, citizenship and faith. These responsibilities can create joys and cause change.

EXPLORING EXPERIENCE

Allow time for individuals to reflect on these questions: What are the major responsibilities in your life? How do you react to these responsibilities? Do you ever experience God or Christ in fulfilling these? How? Share responses in small groups.

EXPLORING THE WORD OF GOD

Choose one of the scripture readings. The primary responsibilities of a Christian are to love God and one another. The two greatest commandments outline this responsibility. Read or proclaim this gospel: Mark 12:28–31 or Matthew 22:24–40.

A catechist or parish member could witness to how they came to experience the love of and for Christ. Invite others to say how they experience the love of God.

Choose one of your major responsibilities. In performing this responsibility, how do you love God? How do you love yourself? How do you love others? Share these reflections with others.

Jesus talks of responsibility in the story of the Good Samaritan. Proclaim this story: Luke 10:25–37. With what character do you identify? Why? Who acts responsibly? What is the key message of the gospel? Invite someone to describe someone they know who is a good samaritan. How has that person influenced others?

PRAYING

Pray slowly together the Prayer of St. Francis. (Before praying a brief description of who St. Francis was may be appropriate.)

GOSPEL CHALLENGE

Reflect on these two questions: How can I better treat others as my neighbors? How can I act more compassionately in my responsibilities, e.g., spouse, friend, citizen, parent, etc.?

CONTROL

Daily newspapers and news reports describe how control is needed in the areas of the environment, drug abuse or violence. Each of us has experienced times when we felt controlled by events and people. The good news of Jesus promises freedom from behaviors, events or people who prevent us from growth.

EXPLORING EXPERIENCE

Reflect on one or two of these questions: How do money, power, possessions or popularity control or influence your decisions? How does your self-control affect others? Do you believe that God controls most events? Why or why not? Write or note your responses. Reflect on these responses in silence. What do they say about who you are?

EXPLORING THE WORD OF GOD

Jesus promises freedom to be in control. Read John 8:31–38. How do you experience the freedom to be yourself in relationship to God and others? Share your response with another person.

In the following story Jesus acts against the popular law and judgment. He delivers the person. Place yourself in the crowd as you listen to this story. Read John 8:1–11. Ask the group to reflect on these questions and be willing to share a response: Have you ever felt trapped or controlled like the woman in the gospel story? What message is being communicated? What kind of person is Jesus? How do you respond to Jesus in this passage?

Ask someone who has dealt with an addiction to tell their story. Invite participants to respond to the story.

PRAYING

We can ask Jesus to free us. Jesus is the great Savior and Redeemer. Reflect on those things or events or persons that control our lives and ask for deliverance.

From all evil	Lord, deliver us
From all sin	Lord, deliver us
From everlasting death	Lord, deliver us
By your death and resurrection	Lord, deliver us
From suffering	Lord, deliver us
From (add your own requests)	Lord, deliver us

Closing Prayer: God you are all powerful and mighty. Help us to trust in you and free us from what controls our growth. Amen.

GOSPEL CHALLENGE

How can I trust in Jesus to help me to be free, to be a better person? What do I need to let go of to follow Christ? How will I respond to violence, drug abuse or other major lack of control in my community?

POWER

EXPLORING EXPERIENCE

Reflect on these questions and share in a small group.

■ What are the ways you have experienced the healthy use of power?

■ How have you experienced abuse of power in your life?

■ All powerful, almighty, all knowing, all loving; these adjectives describe God. How do you respond to each of these descriptions?

■ How have you experienced a mighty God?

EXPLORING THE WORD OF GOD

Jesus told and showed the power of God in his life. Choose and focus on one of these scripture passages: Mark 10:46–52 (Jesus heals blind Bartimaeus) or Luke 18:35–43 (Jesus heals a blind man). After reflection, responses to these questions can be shared. Human beings can be blinded by their own needs, ambitions, or faults. Recall an experience in which you have been blinded. Reflect on this question: How do you respond to Jesus who has the power to heal?

Read Luke 8:40–54 or Matthew 9:18–26 (Jairus' daughter and the woman who touched Jesus' cloak). Are you in need of any healing in your body, emotions, relationships, past? How do you seek the healing power of God?

Luke 8:1–11 (Woman caught in adultery). In this passage, where do you find yourself in the crowd, in the leaders, in the sinfulness of the woman? Why? How have you been affected by the power of God? After reading the above gospel invite someone to speak of experiencing the healing power of God's love. How do you experience the power of God's forgiveness? What do you know of the sacrament of penance?

PRAYING

Jesus says ask and it shall be given. Invite individuals to pray prayers of petition by using this or a similar phrase.

We pray for healing for the sick	*Response:* God, hear us.
We pray for those who suffer from injustice.	God, hear us.
We pray for (add your petitions)	God, hear us.

Closing Prayer: God you are all powerful and caring. Hear these requests and grant them through Jesus Our Redeemer and Savior. Amen.

GOSPEL CHALLENGE

Do you know anyone who is in need of healing and forgiveness? How can you use the power of your own gifts to help that person? How do you abuse your own power? What can you do to change this abuse?

PEACE

EXPLORING EXPERIENCE

Imagine that you are in a quiet, peace-filled place, one that you know, a place you find comforting. Place yourself there and relax. Just breathe deeply and relax. You are waiting. Imagine that God comes to you. God speaks these words "Peace be with you." How do you respond? After a period of silence share this response with another.

EXPLORING THE WORD OF GOD

Begin this session with one of these gospel stories, John 20:19–23, Matthew 28:16–20, or Mark 16:14–18. Ask a catechist to prepare a brief witness about what is the peace that Jesus offers, including an exploration of the meaning of "Shalom". After reflection ask individuals to respond to gospel and the witness. What does God's peace mean to you? How do you experience this peace?

Relax. Take a few deep breaths, close your eyes. Imagine that you believe. God comes to you. Picture God. God speaks these words. "Peace be with you." How do you respond?

PRAYING

Sing together: "Peace is Flowing Like a River" by Carey Landry or "The Peace Prayer" by Bob Dufford (*Glory and Praise* Vol. 1).

Pray a litany for people or nations who are in need of God's peace:
We pray for _____
Response: God give them your peace.
Closing Prayer: Glory Be to the Father.

Another possibility is to pray the Prayer of St. Francis.

GOSPEL CHALLENGE

How do you bring God's peace to others in your family or community? How does the promise of peace affect your life?

FORGIVENESS

EXPLORING EXPERIENCE

The Lord's Prayer says "Forgive us our trespasses as we forgive those who trespass against us." Reflect on these questions: When you have sought God's forgiveness or the forgiveness of another, what happened? What were qualities or characteristics of this forgiveness? How did this experience change your life? Please share the experience or the qualities of forgiveness with another person or persons.

EXPLORING GOD'S WORD

Choose one of these stories of forgiveness: Luke 15:11–32 (the Prodigal Son), Matthew 18:10–14 (Parable of the unforgiving servant), Matthew 18:21–25 (Parable of the lost sheep). Please discuss in small groups:
1) What was your image of Jesus?
2) How did you respond? or How do you respond to Jesus' forgiveness? Have you ever experienced this kind of forgiveness? With whom? How do you practice forgiveness in your life?
A catechist can relate how he or she has experienced forgiveness and how that experience relates to the sacrament of reconciliation. Encourage individuals to discuss how they experience God's forgiveness.

PRAYING

As we reflect on our lives, God, who loves us with everlasting love, gives us the insight to see how we have hurt or injured others. Allow time for reflection and ask people to reflect on these questions: Have I recently hurt someone by my words or actions or have I been hurt by someone? How did these incidents affect others? How can I seek forgiveness? How can I forgive the other? Ask for God's help.

Pray together: God forgive me for my failing. I promise to try to forgive others. I ask for the healing power of your forgiveness. Amen.

GOSPEL CHALLENGE

In your life, who is in need of God's forgiveness? How can you bring God's forgiveness to that person? How are you in need of God's forgiveness?

HAPPINESS

EXPLORING EXPERIENCE

How do you respond to these statements?

- The keys to happiness are . . . .
- I am happy when I . . . .
- True happiness is . . . .

Share these responses in small groups.

EXPLORING THE WORD OF GOD

In the gospel, Jesus describes the qualities of a Christian who seeks eternal life, eternal happiness. Listen to Matthew 5:1–12, or Luke 6:20–23. The meaning of the beatitudes needs to be explored. A catechist can focus on one or two of the beatitudes and explain how they promote happiness.

Describe individuals who live or lived the beatitudes. Participants can be asked to reflect on these questions: How do they understand and practice mercy or justice? How do they understand and practice poverty of spirit or another virtue in the beatitudes?

PRAYING

Pray Psalm 119 by alternating verses.
Sing together, "Beatitudes" by Balhoff and Ducote, (*Glory and Praise,* Vol. 3).

GOSPEL CHALLENGE

Which of the virtues described in the beatitudes do you most need to develop? How will you develop it in your relationships? How will you pursue justice with and for others? How will you pursue mercy or humility?

DEATH

EXPLORING EXPERIENCE

When someone you know has died, how have you viewed and responded to death? When you have visited a funeral home what were your feelings about death and what happens after death? How is God involved in death? Try to identify your own feelings about death. After reflection share your response with two other persons.

EXPLORING THE WORD OF GOD

Proclaim Luke 7:11–17 (the Widow's Son). If you were part of the crowd, what would have been your reaction? Reflect on this statement in the context of God's power over death: "God has visited God's People. Jesus is the Redeemer and Savior."

Read or proclaim, John 11:1–44 (The raising of Lazarus). This story centers on bringing life when there is death. Jesus has overcome death by his resurrection. If you were Martha and Mary how would you have reacted? Jesus offers new life. How does Jesus offer new life to you?

Read Luke 24:1–12: Jesus offers life after death. Catholics believe that you continue to live in a different way after death. What are your images of life after death? A catechist can describe how as a Catholic they view death and the resurrection. Invite participants to respond.

PRAYING

Remember those who have gone before us. Remember those who have died (individuals mention the names of those who have died, e.g., relatives, friends). After all names have been said all pray: Eternal light shine on them. May the souls of the faithful departed through the mercy of God rest in peace.

GOSPEL CHALLENGE

Review your beliefs on death. How does the resurrection of Jesus change or challenge your approach to death? Do you know someone who is dying or suffering from a terminal illness? How can you help them?

ANXIETY

EXPLORING EXPERIENCE

Reflect on one or two of these questions and share your responses in small groups. Before major events or a decision an individual often experiences anxiety. Who causes you anxiety or worry and why? What causes you to be anxious? What does God have to do with anxiety? Name a time when you were anxious. Who was present? What happened?

EXPLORING THE WORD OF GOD

Read the scripture and discuss these questions in groups of two or three. Luke 10:38–42: Mary is reflective. Martha is busy. What kind of person are you? Do you prefer quiet moments or would you rather be busy? Jesus says "Mary has chosen the right thing." How will you choose the right thing? How do you relate to Jesus as described in this story?

Reflect on Romans 8:28–30 or Luke 12:22–31. How do you respond to these words of the gospel? What is Jesus asking of you? How do you experience God's consistent care? A catechist or leader could describe a time when he or she was anxious and how he or she discovered or experienced Jesus. How do you relate to Jesus in this story?

PRAYING

Pray Psalm 33 by alternating verses or Sing together "Be not Afraid" by Bob Dufford (*Glory and Praise,* Vol. 1).

44

GOSPEL CHALLENGE

How do you care for those who are less fortunate than you? Who in the parish or community is in need of God's care? How can you respond? Could you volunteer your time at a soup kitchen or shelter for the homeless or another similar activity? How do you find time alone with God?

HOPE

EXPLORING EXPERIENCE

Hope is a Christian virtue. When you hear people say, "I hope something happens," or "I hope that she meets expectation," what do these phrases mean to you? How would you describe hope to another person? Describe a time when you had no hope. Share your reflection in groups of four or five.

EXPLORING THE WORD OF GOD

Read John 8:12–20; Matthew 28:16–20, or John 12:44–50. When a person is in the darkness of despair or doubt, Jesus offers light, a ray of hope. How do you experience this light of Jesus in your life? Who brings hope into your life? Why? A catechist could describe an incident or person that gave hope to him or her and others. The presence of God can bring hope. "I will be with you all days." How is God present in your life? Where do you find God? (Be specific.) How can I better discover God's presence?

PRAYING

The death and resurrection of Jesus Christ gives us hope. Other signs of God's creation and events in our lives offer us hope. We pause here to remember the people, things, and events that give us hope. The beauty of a sunset, a close friendship, the simple actions of a child are examples. God you have given us life and offer us new life in Jesus Christ. We pause to give thanks for all that gives us hope. (Ask each person to name what has given or gives him or her hope.) Simple response to each statement: *Thank you God.*

GOSPEL CHALLENGE

Identify someone you know who may be depressed or moving into despair. How will you bring hope to him or her? How can you brighten the lives of those who are homeless, starving or hurting? How can you develop trust in God?

DOUBT

EXPLORING EXPERIENCE

Recall a time when you prepared for a major event, e.g., a test, competition, an interview, or a meeting. You probably experienced doubts about how the event would go. Identify the event. What were your doubts about what happened. In small groups share a part of your story and then reflect on this question together: What doubts do you have about Christ? Invite people to raise doubts and others to respond.

EXPLORING THE WORD OF GOD

Listen to or read the story of Thomas, John 20:24–29. Before the gospel is read ask each person to relax and imagine that they are in a boat with others and Jesus is present, and listen to the words of the gospel. How do you identify with Thomas? Reflect on how Jesus is your Lord and God. Respond to this saying, "Blest are they who have not seen and have believed."

Read or proclaim Luke 8:22–25. A catechist can speak of how she experiences Jesus' divinity and humanity. Respond to this question: Where is your faith? How do you doubt God's love and power? What sort of Jesus is this who has power to command and what difference does this Jesus make in your life?

Read Luke 8:22–25. Describe an experience when you doubted God's care or power. How do you experience God's care?

PRAYING

Ask individuals to name a characteristic of God and say these characteristics in a litany:

God you are all powerful . . .
God you are merciful . . .
Jesus you are a healer . . .

Jesus you are the savior of the world . . .
Jesus you are the Son of the living God . . .

To each statement all respond: Lord I believe, help my unbelief.

GOSPEL CHALLENGE

How can you better trust others? Identify one person you need to trust more. How will you develop trust?

TRUTH

EXPLORING EXPERIENCE

Reflect on one or two of these statements and share in small groups. When someone told you the truth about yourself what did you experience? How do you respond to this statement, "We hold these truths to be self-evident: that all men are created equal and that they are endowed by their creator with certain inalienable rights." How important is this statement and its meaning for you?

EXPLORING THE WORD OF GOD

Read John 6:25–40. When you have told the truth in a difficult setting what did it cost you? Jesus says, "I am the way, the truth, and the life . . . the one who believes in me has life." How does the truth that Jesus offers bring life to you? How can truth create life? Find someone to give testimony to how the truth of believing in Jesus has given them new life or renewed a sense of living.

Read John 18:28–38. Jesus talks about the reign of God. The proclamation of God's reign is to speak the truth. What do you believe are the truths about this reign of God? What does it offer and challenge? How does this truth affect how you live? How has the truth of Jesus affected the lives of others?

PRAYING

Pray the Apostles' Creed in phrases. To each phrase respond, "The truth will set us free." I believe in God the Father. All Respond: "The truth will set us free"
or Pray alternatively these Psalm verses, Psalm 119 v 142–160
or To each verse of the Psalm respond: Your truth endures forever.

GOSPEL CHALLENGE

How do you witness to the truth that Jesus is Savior and Redeemer? How do you bring the redeeming love of God to others? Identify the people in most need of the truth of the gospel? How can you help them come to know and experience the truth? How do you share the truth of what you believe with others?

FREEDOM

EXPLORING EXPERIENCE

Choose one of these series of questions, reflect on and then share your reflection with another person.

■ How do you respond to or have you experienced this belief: Jesus, by your cross and resurrection you have set us free.
■ Can you identify an experience when you have been set free? What were you freed from? What were you freed to do or become?
■ Complete these sentences:

I want to be freed from _____

I want to be freed to _____

Why?

EXPLORING THE WORD OF GOD

Read or proclaim Luke 4:16–21. Jesus offers us freedom from captivity and the freedom to become brothers and sisters in one God. Find someone in the community who has been a captive of alcohol, drugs or another sickness or habit and ask them to speak about how God has set them free.

Allow individuals time to reflect and share responses to these questions: How are you in need of God's power of liberation? What do you need to be set free from?

Read or proclaim John 8:1–11. Before reading this gospel describe the place and circumstances; ask to be part of the crowd and listen to this story. As a response to this gospel, someone from the community may tell how they experienced being set free by the sacrament of reconciliation or by someone. Jesus freed this woman from sin and challenged the crowd. How do you respond to Jesus who forgives and frees each of us as he did the woman? Jesus challenged her to be different. How does Jesus ask you to be different or to be free to follow the gospel?

PRAYING

All pray together this Eucharistic Acclamation: *Lord by your cross and resurrection you have set us free. You are the Savior of the world. Amen. Alleluia!*

GOSPEL CHALLENGE

The Gospel of Luke speaks of Jesus coming to proclaim the good news to the poor and to set free the oppressed (Luke 4:16–21). Identify a person or persons who are oppressed. How can you help them to become free?

TEMPTATION

EXPLORING EXPERIENCE

St. Paul said that Jesus was like us in all things but sin. Thus, Jesus was tempted. How would you describe Jesus? Name some characteristics.

EXPLORING THE WORD OF GOD

Read Matthew 4:1–4; reflect and share in small groups. How do you respond to being deprived of what you believe is necessary? How do you respond to the statement of Jesus saying, "You need the word of God to Live"? How does the word of God strengthen and heal?

Read Matthew 4:5–7. How have you tested God? What happened? Why did you test God?

Read Matthew 4:8–11. How have you been tempted to put money and other desires before God? What does it mean for you to live this commandment: "I am the Lord your God. Do not put false gods before Me."

PRAYING

Ask individuals to relax and be mindful of God's presence. Try to imagine Jesus coming to each person and lead them in a process of talking with Jesus about their temptation. Then lead the group in asking Jesus' help. This prayer may end with all saying the Our Father.

GOSPEL CHALLENGE

What is the greatest temptation you face just now? How will you continue to resist?

EVIL

EXPLORING EXPERIENCE

Reflect and share responses in small groups of three.

■ How do you experience evil in the society in which you live? Identify social evils. How have you been affected?
■ How have you been affected by excessive violence, ruthless competition or overuse of drugs and alcohol?
■ How have you responded to the presence of evil?

EXPLORING THE WORD OF GOD

Read Matthew 9:28–34, Mark 5:1–20. Reflect and share on this gospel. These gospels state that Jesus has power over evil. Someone who has suffered the consequences of evil can relate how Jesus has helped them heal or change their life. How do I respond to Jesus who has power over evil?

Read Luke 5:31–37. How do you respond to the statement "Jesus, Son of the Most High God, what do you want of me?" What does God want of you? How do you respond to a Jesus who has power over evil?

Read Mark 9:14–29. How do you respond to Jesus who has the power to cast out evil? "Only prayer can drive this kind out." What do you believe is the power of prayer? How have you experienced this power of prayer?

PRAYING

Powerful and loving God we give thanks for your kindness and
For all of creation . . .
For family . . .
For friends . . .

For food . . .
For birth . . .
For faith . . .

Pause and allow individuals to state the good events or people of their lives.

Invite all people to slowly pray the prayer of Jesus: the Our Father.

Response to each prayer: Give thanks to the Lord for God is good.

GOSPEL CHALLENGE

The gospel challenge is to overcome evil by choosing good. People who are poor, lonely and neglected often suffer from the consequences of evil.

How do you live this command of Jesus? "Go back to your family and tell them how much the Lord has done for you and how kind God has been to you"? Who is in need of kindness and gentleness?

Elizabeth S. Lilly

Introduction to Inquiry Sessions

The following topics are not lesson plans for inquiry sessions. Rather they are brief descriptions of various ways in which team members may work with inquirers. They are illustrations of the process outlined in paragraph 38 of the *Rite of Christian Initiation of Adults*. Each topic is divided into five sections: scenario, questions, gospel, invitation, and team reflection.

The scenarios are just the briefest hints of concrete ways or places in which the issues arise. The topics come from reflection upon the lived experience of the people. The inquirer sets the agenda. They come from listening to the stories and questions of the inquirers as they search for faith and meaning in their lives. The team members' task is to become attentive to the common issues in the lives of those present.

Once the issues begin to surface, the questions are tools to develop and clarify them. By asking questions, more people are drawn into the common reflection. Questions give rise to more questions. The discussion can move from "what" to "why." Participants—inquirers, sponsors, team members, guests—are all invited to look for meaning in the specific experiences of their lives.

The gospel section includes several passages that might speak in a particular way to the discussion. The gospels introduce Jesus, the Son of God, who lived and died for the salvation of the world. This is central to the period of evangelization. This is good news!

The good news is expressed in an invitation to share the living tradition of Christians, the church. The inquirers are encouraged to integrate the faith of the church into their lives. This integration is multi-dimensional. There will be times for sorting and understanding information. There must also be times for developing the images of Christianity. Time, patience and practice are needed for this assimilation. Progress may not be predictable and it may seem that you take two steps forward and one step backward at times. Role models and companions are important.

A "start to the practice of calling upon God in prayer" (RCIA 42) is an important part of the invitation section. The examples given are based on prayers of petition (spontaneous requests for help, Minor Exorcisms, RCIA 94) and prayers of thanks (Grace Before Meals, Kyrie). The prayer is modeled on Jesus' prayer, and the prayer of other Christians.

The period of the precatechumenate is a time for the inquirers to become more aware of the Lord in their lives, and of the church, and to clarify their intentions and desires. The section on team reflection suggests ways for the team members and sponsors to discern this conversion process with the inquirers. Conversion is multifaceted and discernment is ongoing. Regular assessment will assist in the preparation for the Rite of Acceptance into the Order of Catechumens (RCIA 42).

Again, these are not suggested lesson plans. A given topic may be the core of a group's discussion, exploration, and prayer for several weeks. Topics may return again and again depending on the people involved, the season of the year, the life and issues of the particular community. When topics arise repeatedly, there is the opportunity to deepen the discussion. As a small group builds trust, the sharing will move from the level of information to the level of formation. The issues come from the Spirit's urgings in our lives. Tend to them all.

RELATIONSHIPS

SCENARIO

A young man recalled a family reunion that his parents had taken him to when he was fourteen. Of the fifty people present, he only knew his own family, an aunt and uncle, and two first cousins when he arrived. After three days he not only could describe the family tree, but he had new friends among his second cousins from the west, mid-west and south.

A mother reflected on her relationship with her oldest daughter who was a freshman in college. When the mother had been twenty-one, her own mother had died. She did not have the personal experience of the relationship between adult child and parent. She was looking for a model for this relationship.

During the first year in a new town, a woman was busy learning her way around, finding out about the particular customs and opportunities of that community. She met a variety of people. She noticed that the women whom she found most interesting all belonged to the same organization. She soon applied for membership in that group to continue to find companionship and interest groups.

QUESTIONS

How do we define ourselves? What family stories do we tell with pride and which do we prefer to keep hidden?

Family relationships are inherited. What about those which we choose? How do they form us? What does "belonging" mean? What organizations do you belong to?

GOSPEL

Matthew 5:21–26	Reconcile with your brother
Matthew 18:19–20	"Where two or three meet in my name"

Mark 3:31–35	Anyone who does the will of God
John 14:6–10	"To have seen me is to have seen the Father."
John 15:1–8	The true vine

INVITATION

Everybody wants to know "Who am I?" The way each of us answers that question, helps give some meaning to our lives. Each of us is part of a complex network of connections and associations. Among these we tend to nurture a few in particular.

Relationships are not neutral. Some keep us humble, while others are a source of pride. Some tend to limit us, while others challenge us to become more than we presently are.

In the gospels Jesus is always calling us to an awareness of our connectedness, not only with each other but with God. Discuss the saying: "When I looked for God, I came away empty; when I tried to find myself, I became confused: When I found my brother (or sister), I found all three."

Jesus, Son of God, images the most universal human relationship, family. Family is often described as the micro-church. In families there is a sense of presence and connectedness. In families, particularly at times of birth, marriage, and death, anniversaries and reunions, we can come to the experience of the presence of God.

Jesus calls God, "Father." In as many ways that are possible, tell family stories and parish stories and gospel stories together. In many names and phrases, describe our relationship to the God who gives us life, loves us, cares for us, forgives us. We are made in the image of God. Share the stories of how we are generating life in our families and communities, loving, nurturing, and forgiving.

TEAM REFLECTION

How are the inquirers beginning to relate with the Christian community? Do they sense the presence of God in Jesus in the church?

CHOICES

SCENARIO

The mother of four shared the story of a difficult choice that she and her husband made several years earlier. Their first child was born with an open spine and other severe complications. They chose to support him with nourishment, comfort, pain relief and touch, but not to take extraordinary measures to prolong his life. They held him, fed him, sang to him, and rocked him. He died before he was a month old.

A graduate student told of being limited in the choice of schools because of family obligations. She felt that she needed to stay in one particular metropolitan area. Even there, though, she had a choice of several major universities.

An older man told of leaving school after eighth grade to help with the family farm during a depressed economic time.

Areas in your life where you exercise responsibility are also areas where you exercise choice. Are you a supervisor, parent, teacher, or taxpayer?

QUESTIONS

Do you welcome choice? How do you gather information to make an informed choice? How do you face difficult choices?

Whom or what do you consult? How free are you to make choices?

GOSPEL

Matthew 25:31–45	I was thirsty and you gave me to drink
Mark 8:34–38	Conditions for following Christ
Luke 7:18–30	Acknowledging God's will
Luke 8:4–15	Parable of the Sower

Luke 22:39–46   The Agony in the Garden
John 15:14–19   I chose you

INVITATION

Choices are related to action. Consciously or unconsciously we make choices. Christianity calls us to make choices that are informed by the gospel, choices that lead us toward life and to union with those in need and also with God.

Discuss the needs that cry out for change, for new choices. One parish is cooperating with eleven other churches to provide shelter for the homeless. A lot of work and planning, dreaming and struggling went into the plan for each church to offer a hall one month of the year. What are the choices in your neighborhood?

Some choices will entail suffering and change. Choosing always means that we accept or take on one way and reject or move away from another. Choice involves dying to something in order to embrace a new life. In Christian tradition, people are encouraged to make hard choices by the prayer, strength, and faith of a small community. Invite someone who is regularly part of such a small group to share how the small community is an integral part of their life of faith.

TEAM REFLECTION

Train yourselves to observe the choices that the inquirers are making. Regular participation is already a choice to grow in faith and to seek God in Christ.

COMPETITION

The athlete had been favored to win the competition. When the event happened, however, she did not come in first. She reflected that the publicity and attention had distracted her and broken her concentration. She was sorely disappointed and angry because she had spent so many years in training.

From spelling bees to tennis, from running for office to a chess tournament, from play of the hometown team to a music recital, from bidding for a job to a blue ribbon at the county fair, we live surrounded by examples of competition.

QUESTIONS

When does competition encourage creativity and growth, bring out the best in us, and focus the development of a talent? When does it foster a destruction of all that is in the path? When are we so determined to win or better our record that we pursue that goal regardless of the consequences to others and even to ourselves?

GOSPEL

Matthew 20:1–16	Vineyard laborers
Luke 14:7–11	Choosing a seat at the banquet
Luke 18:9–14	The Pharisee and the publican
John 18:28–40	Jesus before Pilate

INVITATION

The gospels call us to balance competition with sacrifice. In other words, we must strive for a balance between our own interests and the good of the community. We must work for others.

Is there someone in your parish who could speak about negotiations which aim for a win/win solution to problems while still achieving good performance for all concerned? Does your parish or school promote community-building games that stress cooperation rather than competition, for the enjoyment and involvement of all? Share these stories and events with the inquirers.

Practice some critical thinking about competition. Compose an "Examination of Conscience" regarding our attitudes and behavior about competition and sacrifice. Invite all to enter into their own honest reflection while the leader reads the questions with pauses. Begin by inviting everyone to call upon God to guide their thoughts.

TEAM REFLECTION

Is there a willingness on the part of all concerned, parishioners and inquirers, to question the strengths and weaknesses of the competitive nature of the North American culture? Is there a shift in the manner of reaching goals from blind competition to cooperation?

RISK

SCENARIO

A young woman fell in love and married a Catholic man. Immediately, her grandparents disinherited her and her own parents did not speak to her for years. Now she is exploring the possibility of becoming a Catholic.

Another woman finds difficulty relating with one of her co-workers. Part of her job evaluation depends on her good working relationship with the other person. She wants to change the situation. She does not know what to do, only that she is ready to take the initiative to change.

Photo images come to mind. A young Chinese man standing in the middle of the street before a column of tanks. A war veteran standing on railroad tracks to block a munitions train.

Every day we live we make choices and choices involve risk.

QUESTIONS

What is at stake? How do I balance security and growth? Are my choices to risk individual or corporate? Do they impact me alone or a family or community? What does that mean to me or to my relationships?

What gives you the courage to take risks—the support of someone who loves you, the personal experience that all growth involves some risk, a strong conviction? What have you risked in being here today? Who else is involved? Who is supporting you, someone in particular, the faith of the whole church?

GOSPEL

Mark 1:16–20	Come follow me
Luke 6:27–35	Love of enemies, lend without any hope of return
Luke 10:29–37	Good Samaritan
John 17:11–19	Prayer of Jesus

INVITATION

We take risks in order to grow. Some may be calculated, based on well-founded trust. Or they may arise out of searching for wholeness and justice. Tell about Francis of Assisi, who risked a traditional way of life and found more meaning and satisfaction.

What does the gospel call us to risk? Team members, inquirers, and guests can share the tension they feel as they examine their lives in the light of the invitations of Jesus. Share the examples of the cost of discipleship.

Encourage each other. Read the Prayer of Saint Francis, and discuss both the hope and the hesitancy that we feel. Invite each one to pray in silence, in his or her heart, for the courage to risk, to change one thing that keeps us from belief.

TEAM REFLECTION

Conversion, turning from the familiar and seemingly secure involves risk. Risk-taking increases with trust. Are we willing to tell our own stories of risk and conversion?

WONDER

SCENARIO

The pope arrived in a country for the first time. As soon as he stepped from the airplane, he knelt and kissed the ground.

The hiker tells of the beauty of the sunset and sunrise in his remote camp.

A young woman tells of her mother's habit of thanking God upon a safe arrival after a journey.

A new father describes his joy and exhilaration at the birth of his first child.

The powerful image of the photograph of the earth taken from space comes to mind.

The awareness of another's love can arouse wonder. Love goes beyond reason, it is not earned or measured.

QUESTIONS

Where do you experience wonder? Is nature a place of wonder for you? Do you feel connected to the wonders of creation?

In how many ways do you ask, "Who am I?"

How aware are we of wonder? Do we experience things as dull and ordinary or do we appreciate the wonders around us?

Does a growing awareness threaten us or bring a new sense of comfort and peace? Do we respond with awe and amazement or with retreat?

GOSPEL

John 15:1–9	Vine and branches
Luke 1:46–55	The magnificat
Luke 8:22–25	Calming the storm
Luke 18:35–43	The blind man at Jericho

INVITATION

Wonder seems to be connected to the awareness of how interdependent we are—with each other, with creation, and with God. Look at ways our church draws our attention to wonder. What, for example, in our prayer and celebration, leads us to the wonderful mystery of the incarnation?

Inquirers may observe things about us, about our prayer, and about our way of living that we have overlooked or taken for granted.

Tell the account of passover, of the Israelites' awareness of God's saving action in their lives. Tell of miracles in Jesus' life and of his dying and rising. Tell of God's constant love and of Jesus who died for the salvation of all.

Response to wonder is gratitude. Begin to address God with prayers of thanks. Share examples of family grace before meals. Sing "Amazing Grace."

Invite guests who have a sense of wonder in their lives, people who treat others respectfully with an awareness of God's love.

TEAM REFLECTION

Do you hear expressions of wonder and gratitude more than complaints of dullness and boredom? Listen and observe ways in which the inquirers begin to sense the presence of God as a wonder in themselves.

SUCCESS

SCENARIO

An engineer visits a children's hospital weekly. One day he spent extra time with a twelve-year-old boy who had cancer. The boy was hard to talk to and had a rebellious attitude, but the man was not put off. The following week when he returned to the hospital, the supervisor had a note for him from the boy's mother. She had asked the staff to tell the man how much her son had appreciated the attention and presence of his visitor.

A bicyclist had set a goal of reaching a summit without stopping to rest or to push the bicycle. On his fourth trip he made it to the skyline road without dismounting.

There are many stories of good news: promotions, graduations, receiving a clean bill of health, meeting goals.

QUESTIONS

How do I define success? What are society's criteria?

What does success mean? Did I deserve it? Did I work for it or fight for it? Does it belong to me alone? What responsibilities are connected to success?

GOSPEL

Matthew 7:15–20	Good fruit
Mark 12:12–22	The rich young man
Luke 5:1–11	The miraculous catch
Luke 18:28–30	Rewards of the disciple

INVITATION

Success can be related to gifts and skill development. The successful teacher teaches well, the successful carpenter builds well. Invite members of the group to share success stories. Often these stories are told in the first person: "I did it." Listen for indications of cooperation and interdependence. Encourage them to recognize that their good fortune involves their work, their hope for the future, and their cooperation with God's will.

Christians believe that God's will will triumph. In the incarnation, the word of God made flesh, Jesus, God is with us. The greatest success in a Christian's life is in the sharing of God's life in Jesus, through the Spirit.

Compare our successes with the life of Jesus. There was frustration with his apparent lack of worldly success. Jesus' success is in living in union with the will of his Father. Jesus constantly prayed that God's will be done. We also pray for this, for ourselves and for the world.

Take a look at the Opening Prayer for Sunday Mass. Again and again, we thank and praise God, and pray that we will be open to God's word, God's will. Only through God's grace can we begin to do this. In paying attention to the church's prayer, we can begin to make it our prayer. Members of the group could begin to rephrase that style of prayer in their own words.

TEAM REFLECTION

Are you aware of the beginnings of calling upon God in prayer, to praise, to give thanks, and to ask for help and direction?

FEAR

A former jet fighter pilot who flew two hundred missions over Vietnam tells of fear keeping him alive. He said that fear heightened his awareness, kept him from distractions.

A mother responds to her elementary school aged son when he asks what to do if shooting ever started in his school. She wants to protect him from fear and feels helpless when she cannot. She tells him to lie very quiet and still if he ever is in such a situation.

We meet people who are facing a medical exam with some fear. They have a suspicion that something is wrong but they are afraid to know the truth.

Sickness, unemployment, death, divorce, being different, all can be the source of fear.

QUESTIONS

How is fear a healthy sign, an early warning? How do I respond to a situation that raises fear for me? Do I seek help? Do I pray? Do I become paralyzed? What is needed to move through fear?

GOSPEL

Matthew 10:26–31	Do not be afraid
Mark 4:35–41	Calming the storm
Luke 12:4–7	You are worth more that hundreds of sparrows
Luke 24:36–43	Peace be with you
John 9:18–23	Parents of the man born blind act in fear

INVITATION

Fear is one of the most powerful forces for action or for inaction. We can be frozen in fear or finally awakened to take positive action. In fearful situations we readily recognize our dependency on God. How can we examine our reaction to fear and how can we hear the confidence and hope of Jesus when he calmed his fears and the fears of others?

Continue to create a trusting environment where people can be free to uncover their fears. Be supportive of one another. Begin the practice of naming the fears in our lives and asking for hope and vision to move beyond them.

Invite someone to share his story of facing a fear by addressing the root cause. This could be someone who was afraid of living in a town with an increasing hunger problem and who now volunteers in the soup kitchen. Or someone who was afraid of people of a different race, but who has participated in a host family program.

Reflect on the presence of the Christ within us, giving us the courage to address our fears, understand them and move through them. Translate these reflections into a prayer modeled upon the Minor Exorcisms (numbers 90–94, RCIA). An example is:

Lord Jesus Christ
 when your disciples were filled with fear
 you came into their midst
 with a message of peace.
Keep us from becoming deaf in our anxieties and fears.
Help us to hear your word of peace.
Do not let us remain troubled.
May we believe in you.
Amen.

TEAM REFLECTION

Observe who can join in praying to be free from fear. How comfortable are the inquirers in calling upon God in prayer? Listen for their stories of recollecting the peace of Jesus and calling for this grace on their own.

LIFE

SCENARIO

A man told of his excitement at the birth of his daughter's first child. A new father describes his experience in the delivery room with his wife as incredible.

A woman told of learning to live independently after years of married life. She describes hectic days, following nights of not enough sleep. She felt the risk involved in her choices, yet she described herself as living a new life.

Ethical questions of today from war, killing of civilians, abortion, euthanasia, mercy killing, to living with dying call our attention to life.

QUESTIONS

What does the dignity of life mean? What does the quality of life mean?

How do we respect life—our life, the life of another?

GOSPEL

Matthew 8:5–13	Centurion's daughter
Mark 8:34–38	Lose life for Christ's sake
Luke 10:29–37	The Good Samaritan
Luke 12:22–32	Trust in God
Luke 15:11–32	The Prodigal Son
John 8:12	Light of life

INVITATION

The invitation of Jesus is to integrate faith in God with everyday living. This is the work of Christian living and it begins with the first steps toward Christian initiation.

All life is a gift. God is the source of life. Our task is to enter as fully as possible into life. One way to focus on this is to become more conscious of the present, to rejoice or grieve, to anticipate or to remember, to listen or to act. In doing this, we also can become more aware of God's presence in our lives. We can grow in trust.

The Christian gathers with other Christians for worship, and for works of charity and mercy. In some parishes, people gather each week of Lent to share a simple supper of soup, bread and beverage. A few people contribute a pot of soup each week. Others contribute what they would have normally spent on dinner to a fund for the hungry. These suppers are called "SOUP: Sharing Ourselves with Undernourished People".

Invite the inquirers to join a parishioner in some action that increases our gratitude for life and contributes to the life and well-being of others.

TEAM REFLECTION

Do you hear the hope or desire for a new life in the comments, questions, reflections, and stories of the inquirers?

GOODNESS

SCENARIO

A man helped an older woman by changing a tire on her car. When he refused any payment, the driver was astonished. He told her, "Do a good turn for someone else, that's payment enough." As she told the story, she conveyed her surprise at the good deed which was unexpected, and which to her was of great value.

In spite of fear, isolation, and danger, people do reach out to others whom they do not know.

QUESTIONS

Where does the spontaneous response to do a good turn come from? How is goodness related to concern for others? Does goodness seek a reward? Is goodness catching? How do I feel when I do something good? How do we learn goodness?

GOSPEL

Matthew 5:14–16	You are the light of the world
Matthew 12:9–14	Cure on the Sabbath
Matthew 13:24–43	Parable of the wheat and the weeds
Luke 6:43–45	Good fruit

INVITATION

Jesus often points to the good results, the fruit of an endeavor to illustrate the breaking in of God's kingdom. What good is coming from your questions and your reflections?

St. Julie used to tell her sisters to repeat over and over, "How good is the good God!" This can become your prayer. In prayer you can name and contemplate the goodness of God. This action, good in itself, is like leaven. Goodness is part will and part heart. It can grow.

Reflecting on our own goodness leads us to wonder at it's source. Recognizing that goodness is more than our own making, we can begin to thank and praise God, the source of goodness. Turn to the psalms for an appropriate spoken prayer to share with the group.

TEAM REFLECTION

It may be easier for us to recognize goodness in another rather than in ourselves. Sponsors could make special note to name and affirm goodness in the inquirer.

INFIDELITY

SCENARIO

A man's word to another, a contract signed, and a partnership began. The lawyer told them that if they ever broke up he would not represent either one since he was friends with both. And, after some years, it happened. One partner locked the other out of the business. There was a violation of the partnership trust. It ended.

There are many personal experiences of divorce, of broken marriage vows. There are stories of promises broken and trust betrayed.

QUESTIONS

What does it mean to be faithful? What does it mean not to act in good faith? What does it mean to give one's heart? What is a broken heart?

Can I keep promises I make, even to myself? Can I stay on a diet? Can I discipline myself to read, write in a journal, keep in touch with friends? Daily, I can meet questions of faithfulness and infidelity.

GOSPEL

John 10:1–21	Good Shepherd
Mark 10:1–12	The question of divorce
Mark 12:23–34	The greatest commandment
Matthew 26:69–75	Peter's denial

INVITATION

We can begin to understand the mystery of God's faithfulness even in the experiences of our own unfaithfulness. We can recognize our desire for the constancy of God's love in these experiences. We can learn to accept God's mercy, to pray for God's mercy and goodness.

The liturgy of the church invites us to experience faithfulness—both in the acts of salvation of God and in our own constant response. Psalms are significant forms of faithful prayer, faithful response. Check the Lectionary or search the psalms yourself for appropriate passages.

Formulate a short litany modeled upon the "Lord, have mercy." Some examples are: "Lord Jesus, you call us to follow you, Christ Jesus, you are the way and the truth, Lord Jesus, you seek us when we are lost."

Invite a couple who participate in marriage enrichment or encounter programs to share the work of living a faithful life in marriage.

TEAM REFLECTION

One of the important tasks is the suitable and faithful explanation of the gospel. In preparation for these meetings, read a whole gospel from beginning to end in one sitting. Renew your own faithfulness to the good news.

Another task is to be faithful to the inquirers, to be available to them and attentive to their questions and needs. Even when things are not clear or when faith seems difficult or absent, their constancy and desire are already a sign of God's grace in them.

LIFESTYLE

SCENARIO

A mother told of her ten-year-old's birthday party. The day came for the party and the invited guests did not arrive. Some phone calls found that they each had forgotten or done something else. The mother quickly gathered some children of different ages, children of family friends and the party was on its way.

On a trip through the southwest, a boy asked his father why there was grass on one side of the road and only mud on the other. After observing this for some time, and even stopping to explore a creek bed, the man concluded that one side had been overgrazed to the point where nothing grew anymore and the land was washing away. He wondered if the profit value of beef had been more important than conservation of the land.

A look through the Sunday newspaper will give a broad picture of lifestyle choices before all of us. Whatever our circumstances, we are part of a consumer society.

QUESTIONS

What are we moving toward, or running from? Are we seeking one goal at the cost of others? What is that cost?

How do we distinguish between needs and wants? How much freedom does an individual exercise in setting a lifestyle?

How often do we talk about how difficult it is to "find time" for all that we want to do? How do we value and weigh all that is before us?

How are our lives structured by our need for comfort and convenience?

GOSPEL

Mark 14:3–9	Anointing at Bethany
Mark 10:28–31	The first shall be last
Matthew 21:28–32	Parable of the two sons
Matthew 22:1–14	Parable of the wedding feast
John 4:5–42	Woman at the well

INVITATION

Who do we know who seems to make wise decisions? Men and women who experienced the Christian Family Movement (CFM) small communities over several years can share their story of consciously choosing their lifestyle. The CFM process of observe, judge, act has empowered these people to evaluate the temptations of our life with gospel values. Over the years they have made choices that affect their lifestyles.

The gospels call us to look beyond a local or national boundary, to common universal qualities in all people. With the information services available to us in North America today, we have a responsibility to see the effect of our consumer lifestyle on the world. Invite someone from the parish who belongs to an international organization such as Bread for the World, Beyond War, or Oxfam to join an evening of sharing and questioning.

When lifestyles are questioned, there could be some discomfort. The leader could invite all to pray for strength. An example, is found in the Minor Exorcisms (number 94 D, RCIA). It could be adapted to reflect Mark 10:28–31.

Lord Jesus Christ,
you promised your followers eternal life.
  Help all of us to hear the word of your gospel,
  and protect us from the spirit of greed,
    of lust, and of pride.

May all who seek you find your blessings.
May all who work for peace and freedom
endure persecution and share the kingdom
  you promise.

May they finally see God in the joy of heaven
where you live and reign for ever and ever.
Amen.

TEAM REFLECTION

Is Sunday worship, the regular hearing of the gospel proclaimed in a community of faith, becoming a pattern in the lives of the inquirers?

Are the inquirers beginning to evaluate the assumed patterns of their lives?

ATTITUDES

SCENARIO

A college student returned home for the summer. She was eager to renew contact with her friends. But she discovered that with one, she could not pick up where she had left off before college. She just explained that the friend's attitude was different. They did not seem to have the same interests anymore.

Changes in our lives, such as a new job or a new neighbor, can call an unconscious attitude to mind. We can become mindful of an attitude, a judgment, prejudice. We become aware of labels and categories.

QUESTIONS

How do we form our attitudes? What do our attitudes say about our values, about what is important to us?

How do we take on a new attitude? How can we begin to take on a Christian attitude? How can we examine our attitudes in light of the gospel?

GOSPEL

Matthew 5:1–12	The Beatitudes
Matthew 9:10–13	Eating with sinners
Mark 2:1–12	Cure of a paralytic
Matthew 12:33–37	By your words you will be acquitted
John 7:16–24	Do not judge according to appearances, but according to what is right.

INVITATION

An attitude might be compared to a lens; it colors everything we look at. Attitudes are carried as images in our imagination. If we want to become aware of Christian attitudes, we need Christian images.

Invite someone to your group who is able to lead an imaging prayer.

Develop a collection of slides. In one parish the Catechetical Director makes a slide show every year of the Confirmation and First Communion candidates. Something like this could be part of a session. Another person, a former photography student, has a slide meditation of the resurrection. Look around your community for the gifts you need.

Examine the beatitudes. What does "poor in spirit" mean? Proclaim the passage prayerfully, with pauses. Ask aloud for the grace to hear as Jesus intends you to hear these words.

TEAM REFLECTION

Who has changed an attitude? Who can tell a story that begins: "I used to . . . but now I . . ."

Listen for the change in the inquirer's language from, "Why do you . . ." to "Why do we . . ." Be attentive for the signs of a change of attitude, a conversion.

WEALTH

SCENARIO

Casual conversation touched on the subject of the state lottery. Everyone dreamed about what he or she would do with the winnings. Some people took the topic lightly, but it seemed that some were quite serious about the pursuit of more and more money and prizes in their lives.

The newspaper carried a story of a family that needed to build onto and remodel its home. The family has ten children, all adopted, all with handicaps, eight in wheelchairs. The parents describe themselves as poor in money but rich in love.

A couple's car carries the bumper sticker, "I owe, I owe, so off to work I go." The accumulation of wealth is a popular goal. Most often this is translated into money and financial security. There may be stories of the lack of monetary wealth. There are stories of wealth in friendship, good health, and good fortune in all aspects of life.

QUESTIONS

Is wealth a controlling factor of our lives? Do we idolize wealth? Are we consumed with seeking wealth?

Or is wealth an invitation to generosity? Is monetary wealth necessary for generosity? What responsibilities are associated with wealth?

GOSPEL

Mark 10:17–22	Rich young man
Mark 10:23–27	Danger of riches
Matthew 6:19–21	True treasure
Matthew 25:14–30	Talents
Luke 12:16–21	On hoarding possessions

Luke 16:9–13   Detachment from riches
Luke 18:18–27   The rich aristocrat

INVITATION

The gospels invite us to a new life that cannot be purchased. This new life is a gift of God. This life is described as a kingdom which brings to mind all sorts of riches and treasure, peace and security.

Listen for expressions of the human desire for these. Seek to give examples of people who have a strong trust in God that gives a foundation to all their other endeavors. Invite parishioners from all walks of life to be guests at your gatherings. Ask them to share why their faith is important to them.

Another guest could be someone who works closely with a parish or diocesan out-reach program or with Catholic Charities. Discuss how wealth and resources are shared.

The greatest wealth is God's love, freely given to us. Read a portion from chapters 14 through 17 in the Gospel of John and invite all to meditate on this gift of immeasurable value.

TEAM REFLECTION

Do you hear indications of people beginning to change their lives in the areas of the pursuit and use of wealth?

Elizabeth Harubin Sinwell

Introduction to Inquiry Sessions

The following 13 topics are designed as resources, rather than as lesson plans, for meeting with inquirers. It is intended that the resources will help to focus the various topics around real-life experiences and help the parish respond to the questions, concerns and needs of the inquirers themselves.

Each topic or session is organized as follows:

Considerations. This section identifies, enlarges upon, and uses examples of the topic. It ends with questions for reflection, preparation, or discussion for times with inquirers.

Scriptures. This section identifies scripture passages which relate to the topic and recommends specific methods which might be used to share the message. Several passages or groups of passages are given—catechists need not use all the suggestions given, but should choose freely, guided by the needs of the inquirers, the abilities, talents and preferences of the catechists, and the promptings of the Spirit.

Reflection/Action. This section provides discussion and reflection questions and suggestions for possible actions inquirers and catechists may engage in in response to the topic's challenges.

Prayer. This section presents various prayer forms which might be used before, during, or after sessions.

FAMILY

CONSIDERATIONS

The so-called "traditional" family still exists—mother, father, children. Alongside these are a host of other kinds of families—extended families, blended families, one parent and step-parent families, adoptive and foster families and every other combination that takes shape. Actually, the variety seen now is probably more like what has existed over the centuries than what we have come to call the "traditional" family.

What is basic to the experience of family is not so much a biological connection, but an intimacy, commitment, or faithfulness among the members. And so we hear "family talk" where no biological or even matrimonial or cohabitational bond exists—the man "who was like a brother to my father," or "I feel closer to you than to my own sister." We see Mother's Day greeting cards printed for the "woman who is like a mother to me."

1. What was/is your family like? What are the bonds that keep you together? What are the issues that cause alienation?
2. Is there a person to whom you are not related whom you consider as close to you as any family member could be or is? If so, describe your relationship with that person.
3. What does family mean to you? Are your hopes for family realistic?

SCRIPTURE

Reflect on Ephesians 3:14–21. Consider how this reading describes what we wish for members of our families (including parish families and the family of humanity). A youth or other member of the parish might describe a personal vision of what true family can be. Inquirers can also be encouraged to have and share visions and dream dreams.

Read the story of the Prodigal Son (Lk 15:1–32). Consider the perspectives and feelings of each of the characters in the story. With whom do you most identify? Have you ever had a similar experience? Why do families celebrate together? What about people like the older son who sulk and complain or are self-righteous? A catechist might share these questions and thoughts.

Read and reflect on John 17:9ff, Jesus praying for the disciples and all believers. What kind and degree of connectedness does this passage speak of? What examples from one's own experience illustrate the power of the passage? Catechists might share the feelings and challenges the passage elicits from them.

REFLECTION/ACTION

1. Is it easy for you to think of God as a parent or Jesus as a sibling? Why or why not?
2. All people are God's children. Do you consider yourself part of a global family? Why or why not? What implications and challenges does your response present to you?
3. Is there someone in your life from whom you feel alienated? How might you reach out to that person? Try it. (If you already have, try again or a new way.) Ask Jesus for help.
4. Is there a member of your family who has faith in Jesus the Christ? Ask that person about faith and family.

PRAYER

> Read John 14:13–14.
> Pray for the needs of the members of your family.
> Pray together the Lord's Prayer.

GOD

CONSIDERATIONS

God is like . . .

A big old man hurling lightning bolts. ("Gotcha!")

An executive at a world-wide lottery. ("Her number was up.")

A traffic engineer calculating the errors of unsuspecting motorists. (Again, their "number was up.")

A chief of medicine allowing little children to suffer. ("I can't believe there's a God, with all the suffering in the world.")

A tough taskmaster (or a harsh father) doling out punishments for transgressions, for one step out of line. ("God is punishing him.")

A strategist or CEO making the "inside" arrangements for us, not them. ("God is on our side.")

An agency bureaucrat waiting to give aid to those poverty-stricken, disease-ridden populations if only they would use their own bootstraps. ("God helps those who help themselves.")

An astute savings and loan officer approving personal or national wealth. ("We must be doing what God wants; look at our affluence.")

The list goes on and on. Believer or not, pious or skeptic, reflective or flippant, significant or petty, young or old, we each carry within ourselves an image of who God is supposed to be, of what we believe God is responsible for, of who God is.

What is your image of God? What was your image of God when you were a child?

What has influenced you in how you perceive God? Why?

Do you think people's ideas about God are mere projections of themselves? Are they helpful or burdensome? What about your own ideas of who God is?

SCRIPTURE

Read Luke 9:18–20. How do people in general (or people you know) think of God? How do personal experiences, knowledge, age, other people, unusual circumstances affect how you think of God? How is Jesus indicative of who God is? What are the meanings of the expressions "Messiah of God" and "Son of God"? (One catechist might prepare a brief explanation of the term "messiah"—its occurrence in history in general and in the Bible specifically; also, an explanation of the meanings of the title "Son of God." A good study aid for the scriptures would be a useful resource.)

The following scriptural passages are helpful in reflecting on who God is and pointing to Jesus:

- images of shepherd (Ps 23:1, 80:1; Is 40:11; Jer 31:10; Jn 10:1–21; Hb 13:20);
- images of sustainer and creator (Gen 1–2; any psalms on the topic; Is 40:28–31);
- the word and work of Jesus (Mk 9:2–8; Jn 5; Jn 6:44f; Jn 12:44–50; Jn 14; any of the catechists' favorites);
- like a hen gathering her chicks under her wings (Mt 23:37–39);
- like a father giving good things (Mt 7:7–11);
- the lost sheep (Mt 18:10–14);
- the lost coin (Lk 15:8–10);
- blessing the children (Mk 10:13–16);
- by extrapolation from the parables of the reign of God.

One or more catechists might relate how one or a few of these passages illustrates for them what God is like.

A member of the parish might witness to an event or series of events in which she or he perceived God in a new way.

REFLECTION/ACTION

1. "God is love" (1 Jn 4:16). What does this mean to you? What implications does it have?
2. How does knowing who Jesus is help you to know who God is?
3. How do your beliefs about God relate to your notion of death?
4. How is God like—or different from—"The Force" in *Star Wars*?
5. Have a discussion about God with someone you care about. Or write a letter.
6. What difference does believing in God make? Explain. Do you know anyone whose belief in God you admire? What difference does it make in his or her life? What difference can/does it make in yours?

7. God is at the center not just of the spectacular moments but of the *ordinary* times of our lives. Do you agree? Why or why not?

PRAYER

Leader: O God, open my lips
Response: And my mouth shall declare your praise.
Reader: Psalm 121
Leader: O God, open my lips
Response: And my mouth shall declare your praise.
All: Amen. Alleluia!

WORK

CONSIDERATIONS

Work: Devising a wonderful new process at work. Throwing in another load of laundry. Sitting through another disorganized meeting. Sewing together the last of the layers of the quilt. Succeeding in gathering people together around a worthwhile cause. Soldering the 40th clip. Mowing the lawn. Getting right every order the customers made. Finally getting the last of the rocks out of the field. Getting familiar with the new software. Coming in last on the quota.

Some work is creative and exhilirating; some is drudgery or hard labor or both. In some work, the connection to the good of society is clear. Some work seems meaningless. And some work is necessary over and over and over again.

Psychologists and others tell us that through work we experience our dignity. The depression which haunts a person who was fired or laid off for a long period of time is a good example of the loss of that dignity. We feel worthwhile and creative through work. Is there some connection here with the emerging and differing roles of women and men in contemporary society? Yet work also includes the monotonous or unceasing qualities of what we call toil and suffering. Even the concept of injustice is related to our understanding of work. Consider the head of a household who labors 16 hours a day only to provide a bare subsistence or less for the family.

1. What kind of work (maybe your job, but not just your job) do you do? How do you feel about it? Why?
2. In what ways does your work give you a sense of dignity? Explain.
3. If you could choose for yourself one kind of work, of all the work in the world, what would it be? Why? What does your answer say about you?

SCRIPTURE

The Bible consistently deals with real-life problems, situations, struggles, and circumstances. Of course, then, work is an integral part of its testimony from Genesis on. In the Hebrew scriptures there are doctors, judges, craftspersons, blacksmiths, farmers, sailors, etc. In Jesus' parables, too, there is constant reference to work: shepherd (Jn 10:1–6), sower (Mk 4:1–9), servant (Lk 12:42–48), steward (Lk 16:1–8), merchant (Mt 13:45–46), householder (Mt 13:52), a woman kneading dough (Mt 13:33), and harvesters (Jn 4:35–38), are examples. A catechist might relate the kinds of work he or she performs and witness to its meaning for life's journey, including how the work alters things or society as well as its effect on personal development.

Work has several connotations in the light of the scriptures:

a. Work is participation in the creative power of God the Creator. A catechist might witness to some work which contributes to the upbuilding of the realm of God.

b. Jesus of Nazareth was himself a worker (Mk 6:1–3). Not only does Jesus preach a gospel of work, but he himself is a man of work. God is described as working to create the world (Gn 2, Rv 15:3). Jesus participates prominently in that work, and we too are called to take on that particular aspect of our being made in the image and likeness of God. Catechists might witness to a work they perform in response to their being followers of Jesus.

c. All work is linked with toil and is reflective of the cross and resurrection. Sweat and toil put us in union with the cross. And it—and also its fruit—puts us in the center of the resurrection, co-creating the new heavens and the new earth (Rv 21:1), the toil contributing to new good, often increasing human dignity, siblinghood, and freedom. One or two catechists might explain the dual aspects of their work, i.e., how the work is related to both the cross and the resurrection.

(Using John Paul II's *Laborem Exercens* as a resource would be very helpful if an inquirer is particularly interested in this topic.)

REFLECTION/ACTION

1. What aspects of your work are creative? dehumanizing? Why?
2. Do you think there are in today's world any forms of work, or any jobs, that Jesus would not perform? Why or why not?

3. Many people are afraid to become involved in work aimed at social involvement or community progress. How do you deal with the challenge of such work?
4. Is there a work you often considered volunteering for, yet never, or only once or twice, did? Do you think Jesus is calling you to get involved with some specific thing?
5. Why do you think work is linked with redemption and salvation?

PRAYER

Sit quietly for a while.

A leader might guide the others—who remain silent—through quiet and simple reflection on work: its rewards . . . its sorrows . . . its heaviness . . . its fruits . . . its toil and suffering. . . .

Close by carefully reading Matthew 11:28–30.

FAITH

CONSIDERATIONS

Tim, a young adult, is at a faith-seeking point in his life. He has had a serious illness and various surgeries; he has been involved in a car accident in which the injuries to the other person were severe; his good friend was killed in another car accident. Tim is searching for answers, for understanding, for reasons for his own existence. Tim often feels lost, like a sheep.

Usually we do not think about faith until there is a problem. Faith, like trust, becomes an issue when life is dark or there is trouble. During our life's journey, we encounter times that jar us from our routine, from our certainties or our prejudices or judgments, from our comfort. These are the times that require faith. It is in these times that we search for answers, for understanding, for reasons. It is in these times that we often feel isolated, alone, lost.

1. What is occurring in your life right now that causes you pain and that you do not understand?
2. What do you have faith in?
3. When you are in the midst of hard times, what do you do? How do you respond to others in their hard times?

SCRIPTURE

The scriptures are full of stories of the important times of life. They are full of the stories of persons' crises of faith. Read and reflect on the questions for one or more of the following:

a. Mt 9:18–31, Mk 2:1–12, 3:7–12, 8:22–26, Lk 7:1–10, or 9:37–48a about faith bringing healing. Consider Jesus' concern for those who are sick. How do you relate to those who are sick or dying? How do you handle yourself being sick?

b. Mt 8:23–27 or 14:22–33 about faith casting out fear. What fears are irrational or unfounded? What are you afraid of? What fears might Jesus relieve?

c. Mt 15:32–39 or Mk 8:10 about faith in relation to our needs. How have your needs been filled? Have you ever gone hungry or without shelter? With what has God provided you?

d. Mt 17:20 or Lk 17:5–6 about the power of faith. How do you witness to the power of faith in your life? What have you overcome through the power of some form of faith?

Use discussion and personal experience to illuminate the significance of faith.

REFLECTION/ACTION

1. People have faith in all sorts of things. Name some. Are they worthy of faith? Why or why not?
2. Some people say faith is a "crutch." Do you agree? Why or why not?
3. Consider a hard time or crisis in your life. How might Jesus comfort you or challenge you?
4. Do you know a person whom you consider to be faith-filled? How do you know? What is that person's faith? Do you admire it? Talk with that person about faith.
5. What are you afraid of? How might faith in Jesus affect your fear(s)? What can you do to be free from fear?
6. Can you think of anything for which faith would not make a difference? Explain.
7. Think of something difficult, that you know you should do. Do it. Have faith.

PRAYER

Read Psalm 89. Sing "Isaiah 49," or "Take, Lord, Receive."

JUSTICE

CONSIDERATIONS

When we think of justice, many, many images come to mind. We may think of ourselves and who did or didn't do what in our regard. Some of us in Western society think of pay scales and benefits, who has the best or biggest, what we can buy, where we can travel to, what can be mine if I play my cards right.

Yet we all know, too, that justice has a much deeper meaning than this alone. Justice has to do with orphans and widows and strangers. It has to do with the very foundations of human society. Scholars on the subject claim that the greatness of a society is measured not by the well-being of the rich, but by the situation of its most marginal members. In our time working for justice includes working for civil rights, women's rights, gay rights, the rights of the unborn, prisoners, those living in poverty, the handicapped, the dying, the defendant and the victim, the minimum wage, against the arms race and against consumerism, for saving the oceans and the air and the rain forests. . . . The list is long and continues to grow longer as people grow progressively more aware of the needs and injustices surrounding them. A source of hope is the fact that the lists point to a fundamental issue: that we the people of the earth are indeed seeking—personally, locally and globally—justice.

1. Consider injustices that exist. Which injustices disturb you the most? What do your choices tell you about yourself? about your priorities?
2. Why do you think possessions (or other distractions) become so important to people? What possessions do you believe you could not live without?
3. Think globally; act locally. What does the slogan mean to you?

SCRIPTURE

A sense of justice pervades the scriptures. The Hebrew scriptures are literally filled with descriptions, directions, and admonitions concerning justice, the poor and widows, orphans, and strangers. (See for examples, Ex 16:17–21; Lv 25:10, 23; Dt 15:1–6, 12–18; Ps 9:9, 10:17–18, 12:5, 102:20, 107:4–6, 113:7, 118:7, 140:12; Pr 14:31, 22:23, 30:8–9; Is 3:12–15, 5:8–10, 25:4, 61:8; Am 2:6–7, 3:10, 4:1, 5, 6:1–7.) Growing directly from this tradition is Jesus and the good news. His teaching reveals a powerful intensity of single-mindedness and commitment to the seeking of justice. A member of the parish's social action committee might witness to seeking justice using one or more of the following as a biblical base:

a. On possessions and the poor and needy:
- Mt 5:1–12 (beatitudes)
- Mt 6:24 (cannot love God and money)
- Mt 25:31ff (Last judgment)
- Mk 8:36 (gain the world, destroy self)
- Lk 4:18 (glad tidings to the poor)
- Lk 6:20ff (Sermon on the plain)
- Lk 9:10–17 (multiplication of loaves . . . providing for needs)
- Lk 14:12ff (the poor at the banquet)
- Lk 16:19ff (Lazarus and the rich man)
- Lk 19:24–25 (camel through eye of needle)

b. On position, hypocrisy, and judgment:
- Mt 6:1ff (hypocrites' behavior)
- Mt 7:1–5 (plank in own eye)
- Lk 11:39–52 (Woe to you . . .)
- Lk 14:7–11 (the one exalted will be humbled)
- Jn 8:1–11 (woman caught in adultery)

c. Gospel challenges:
- Mt 5:38ff (turn the other cheek)
- Mt 12:1–8 (mercy is required)
- Jn 13:1–17 (washing of feet)

REFLECTION/ACTION

1. Do you believe God is an advocate for the poor? How does our society respond to and interpret poverty? What would Jesus' message be?

2. Why do you think some people use such time and effort to acquire possessions? What do you delight in?

3. Do something for the poor this week.
4. How is the arms race a sin against the poor?
5. What is wrong with sexism, nationalism, consumerism, racism? What would Jesus' message be?

PRAYER

Dim lights, candle, Bible, music in background (e.g., "Seek Ye First," "Be Not Afraid," "Earthen Vessels," "One Bread, One Body").
Silence.
Alternate lines of the Sermon on the Plain (Lk 6:20–25).
Silence.
Pray the Song of Mary (The Magnificat).

HEALING

CONSIDERATIONS

Healing is a lot like reconciliation. It is a kind of getting things back together again, the way they should be.

We can look out into our family, our community, our world, or into ourselves to see a need for healing and to see healing as a reality.

Healing may be physical or psychological or emotional or relational.

Sometimes we look in the right places for healing; sometimes we do not. Sometimes we are healed in ways we never expected. Sometimes healing occurs and we do not even notice it.

Doctors, nurses and pharmaceutical companies do it. Families do it. Friends do it. Even pets and teddy bears can sometimes do it. Often healing is the result of hard work and discipline. And frequently it comes with tears or long, long conversations. Courageous statespersons have even healed relations among nations. And indeed prayer does it.

1. Think of a time you have been healed. How did it happen?
2. Did you ever help heal someone by your presence or words or action?
3. What inside of you needs healing? What about the people you love?
4. Have you ever experienced, or do you know of an incident, in which healing occurred unexpectedly?

SCRIPTURE

There is a common underlying source for all healing. And that source is the healing power of God, given out for us all, and made clear to us through the healing power of Jesus the Christ. (All good things are from God; healing is from God.)

Reflect on the unexpectedness of healing for the sick man at the pool of Bethzatha in John 5:1ff. Does Jesus always have to be asked in order to heal? A parish catechist might share stories of healing heard while teaching.

Read about Jesus' promise of living water for all who are thirsty in John 7:37–39. How is water a healing agent? How is the Spirit active in healing in the local community? Members of the parish might talk about the thirsts they have had in their lives and how they have been able to drink from Jesus' fountains of living water.

Read two or three of the following: the healing of a leper in Mk 1:40–45; many sick healed in Mt 8:16–17 and Lk 6:17–19; the healing of the paralytic brought through the roof in Lk 5:17–26; the widow's son in Lk 7:11–17; and the healing of the blind man in Mk 10:46–52. A member of the parish might witness to a story of renewed health or well-being and the role of God and the community in the healing.

REFLECTION/ACTION

1. In the gospels, healing is very often associated with the forgiveness of sins. How are sickness and sin alike? How do they differ? Why does forgiveness have healing power?
2. All healing is from God, even in the care of an atheist physician, for example. Do you agree or disagree? Why?
3. Why do people pray for healing? Do you? Why or why not? If you do, does it work?
4. Do you know anyone who is or has been seriously ill? What do they pray for? How might you be part of their healing? If there is someone you know who is sick now, visit that person.
5. Why is healing such a large part of the proclamation of the good news of the gospel.

PRAYER

Sing "Peace is Flowing Like a River," including the verse with "healing."

Read: O God, in Jesus you have taught us to look to you in all our infirmities, and to be ministers of healing. We believe in the healing power flowing from your Spirit and ask you now to heal all our wounds . . . (pause) . . . and the wounds of those we love . . . (pause) . . . and the wounds upon this earth . . . (pause). We believe that through your healing power we are free again to be whole and to restore wholeness to the deserts of this world.

Repeat "healing" verse from above song, or sing "Here I am, Lord."

TRUST

CONSIDERATIONS

We learn lessons in trust right from the start. Infants trust the arms of their parents. Toddlers trust that a kiss will make it all better. Children trust their teachers and adolescents both hesitantly and adamantly trust their friends.

We trust traffic signals. We trust that the electricity will be there for the coffee pot, the bus will make its usual stop, and our good friend will be late, as always.

We trust that the sun will rise in the morning, that nature will follow the seasons, the tree out front will eventually shade the house, and most likely one's lungs will continue to breathe while one sleeps.

All these wonderful, ordinary things most of us trust easily and automatically.

The surprises, the struggles about trust come, then, when it is not so easy, not automatic—when we consider or are confronted with parts of our own personal lives, fearing that the mountains may indeed fall, that our own world is falling apart.

We like to think of ourselves as strong, trusting in our abilities, our luck, our looks, our connections, our education, our health— whatever. And when we fail, or are confronted with serious illness or death, or even a sense of our own limitations, we are devastated. We think we have nowhere to turn.

1. In what do you place your trust? Why?
2. Name three people whom you trust. Are there any limitations to that trust?
3. Is there a specific person or thing in which you wish to place your trust but have not? Why?

SCRIPTURES

In Mt 6:25–34 Jesus tells us we have nothing to fear or to worry about. We may place complete trust in God, who will always care for us. A catechist might witness to an experience of trusting in God's care in the face of adversity or uncertainty.

To trust is often a challenge. When our lives are filled with fear, Jesus reminds us of the trustworthiness of our God. Read Lk 12:4–7 and ask a parishioner to tell how worries may be replaced by trust.

Psalm 46 reminds us that our God will never fail us. Like Jesus (see Mt 26:36–46), we can trust, take courage, be still, and know that God is God. Catechists and members of the parish might compile a list of all the times they have experienced the trustworthiness of God and share the list with inquirers.

In Lk 11:9–13 Jesus tells us to ask, to seek, to knock, for we can trust in God's response who, like a parent to the child, gives only good things to us—a fish, not a snake, an egg, not a scorpion. A catechist might relate a story of asking for and receiving good things from God.

REFLECTION/ACTION

1. At this time in your life, what requires a good deal of trust on your part? How do you deal with it? What might Jesus bring to it?
2. Recall the life of an older family member. Did any of your family members ever place their trust in God? How might *you* place your trust in God?
3. Are there persons whose ability to trust you admire? How do they manage to trust? Ask them.

PRAYER

Join hands and slowly pray the Lord's Prayer.

LOVE

CONSIDERATIONS

Love. It means and has meant many different things to many people over time—romantic, filial, erotic; sacrificial, poetic, inspiring; sometimes trivial or shabby.

Yet . . . still . . . love is yearned for.

What, in your opinion, is an accurate example of love?

Have there ever been/are there abuses, atrocities, or other negative deeds performed in the name of so-called love? Explain.

What is love? How do you experience it?

SCRIPTURE

Read Jn 15:12–13. What does it mean to love one another? How do *you* lay down your life for another? How have people laid down their lives for you? (Think about it.) A catechist's story of witness would be appropriate.

Read and reflect on 1 Cor 13. Turn into questions each of the statements of the chapter and respond to them—quietly, thoughtfully, truthfully, mercifully. Catechists might witness to an example of the gift of love in their own lives.

Read 1 Jn 4:7–21. Reflect on its meaning, quietly, patiently. How does God love you? Does Jesus exhibit God's love for you? How are you called to love others? (one, five, many, indiscriminately?) How is the Spirit's presence made known to you? Do you abide in, live in, God? Why or why not? Are you usually fearful, or not? Why? How has Jesus loved you? Is love everlasting? A catechist might lead an experience of centering on God's love, using the above questions.

REFLECTION/ACTION

1. Which of the questions from the scripture section are difficult for you to respond to? Which ones are easy? Why?

2. How have you ever laid down your life for another? Why? What does your response tell you about yourself? about God?
3. How are Jesus' life, death, and resurrection examples of loving? Have you ever participated in such love? If so, when and why? If not, why not?
4. Reflect on 1 Cor 13. Challenge yourself. . . . Congratulate yourself. . . . Rest in God's love for you through Jesus the Christ. Take time to do this each day for a week.

PRAYER

Choose from among the following (to sing or listen to):

- "Though the Mountains May Fall"
- "You Are Near"
- "Here I Am, Lord"
- "The Love of God"
- "Whatsoever You Do"
- "Wherever You Go"
- "I Have Loved You"
- "On Eagle's Wings"
- "Sing to God a Brand New Canticle"

Bring in personal photos, photographs from magazines, etc., that exemplify the songs you have chosen. Prepare ahead a spoken prayer and allow time for personal petitions or responses.

SUFFERING

CONSIDERATIONS

Suffering is part of life. Each of us has no difficulty calling up examples of many kinds of suffering—the anguish of waiting, a friend's brain tumor, a relative's devastating injuries, a child with leukemia, the trouble or loss of someone we love, fire, loneliness, facing the consequences of a poor decision. . . . We can go on and on.

Some people even "get good at" suffering; they "wear it well"; they enjoy it. Some seem to choose to be unhappy, to never accept reality, to never be satisfied, to suffer. Some refuse to be happy.

Yet in every incidence of real suffering, happiness—even joy—can be found.

Peg and her daughter, often at odds with one another, were struggling to have a relationship. Following her daughter's death in a car accident, Peg told of the individuals who are now renewing their efforts to reach out to alienated family members. Peg relates this with tears of joy in her eyes.

Diagnosed with cancer, a man finally finds time to be with his children and wife.

1. Recall a time of suffering in your life. What was the unhappiness in that suffering? What is the happiness to be found?
2. What is your greatest burden right now? How do you deal with it?
3. Is there something you *choose* to suffer? to be unhappy about? Why or why not?

SCRIPTURE

Suffering can indeed turn to joy. A woman's labor pain gives way to joy at birth (see Jn 16:20–22). A parishioner who recently gave birth might recount her story of waiting, of pain and joy.

Read an account of Jesus' passion and death from a gospel. A parish member, reflecting on the story, could tell how personal suffering, or the suffering of a loved one, is united with Jesus' suffering and is redemptive. (See also 2 Tm 2:8–13.)

Suffering is part of the discipline which leads to holiness. Hebrews 12:5–13 advises us against being weak-kneed or droopy and calls us to take strength in God's care for us. Romans 8:17ff assures us that suffering and glory are connected, that nothing can ever separate us from God's love for us, made visible in Jesus. Matthew 16:24 states that following Jesus includes picking up one's cross. A catechist might witness to his or her own suffering that has become a cause of personal growth or intimacy with Jesus.

REFLECTION/ACTION

1. Has another person's suffering ever benefited you? Tell that person and thank him/her.
2. How might your suffering be united with Jesus'?
3. Recall a time of suffering. What good or joy came or might come from it?
4. What do you consider the greatest suffering or pain in the world today? How can you personally reach out to or affect that suffering? Do it.

PRAYER

Sing "Romans 8." (You might explain why the song has its title.)

CHANGE

CONSIDERATIONS

We have all experienced change—many, many times—in our lives. Some changes are obvious: a birth, a graduation, a heart attack, moving to a new place, taking on a new endeavor. Other change creeps up on us so quietly that we hardly experience it as change at all. We grow, we mature day to day, year to year. At first we hardly notice that maturity, those gray hairs, or that children have reached a significant new stage in their lives, or that our perspective on some things has shifted, or that someone we love is somehow different. What is it that awakens us, at last, to notice this change? And why is it that some changes are so pleasant or seem good and other changes seem to disturb us way down deep inside ourselves?

Change is the way we—or another, or nature, or whatever—"go" from one moment to another. It is the way we grow—often slowly and imperceptibly, sometimes spectacularly and quickly. We perceive that we are like clay, being molded, taking form, being fired—shaped by events, relationships, circumstance, moments of clarity or confusion, by our approach to life. In moments of centeredness or crisis, we come to realize the significance of change in our lives and wonder about the things of the universe and come to terms with our own place in this creation.

1. What is changing in your life right now? Do you think you will weather it well? Why or why not?
2. Why are moments of crisis (e.g., medical emergency, international incidents, a family "blow-out") seen usually from a negative perspective and seldom with an eye toward the positive change that could result?
3. Reflect on your life. List some things you thought you would never be able to do, e.g., lose weight, a new skill, speak in front of a group, but that now are easy or second-nature. Do you have any new ones in mind? What are they?

SCRIPTURE

The scriptures often refer to the reality and perception of change in life and nature, that it is God who is the potter, we the clay, the work of God's hand (Is 64:7-8). A parish member might share how an experience of a course of events is seen as being orchestrated by God. (See Jn 14:1-7.)

In 2 Cor 3:16-18, Paul reflects on change in our lives, our transformation into the image of Jesus, our being led by God, that changes have a purpose. (See also Ps 51:12-19.) Youth from the parish might witness to their sense of God's purpose for their lives being shown to them through a youth group, retreat, or outstanding experience.

In the stories of the woman caught in adultery (Jn 8:3-11) and the rich young man (Mk 10:17-31), the call to conversion, to change, is clear. One or two catechists might relate the changes that came into their lives as a result of deep faith in Jesus.

REFLECTION/ACTION

1. Draw a time line of your life. Mark important dates and significant happenings. Do you see change? Do you see any patterns? How might Jesus be calling you?
2. Name two things in your life that have changed, that you have gone through, and of which you can now see the value for your life. Name two that you realize were/are insignificant or self-destructive.
3. Why do you think change is often so difficult? How might one see change through the eyes of faith?
4. Jesus calls us to changes in our lives, to growth, to transformation. One way we are transformed is through sensitivity and service to others. Think of a person you know who is going through a difficult change. Give that person a call on the telephone.
5. Which of your plans is going wrong? How might God be surprising you?

PRAYER

Gather near a candle and Bible.

Write on a small piece of paper a word, phrase or drawing to describe a change you are experiencing now and through which Jesus might be calling you to new life. Fold the paper and hold it loosely in the open palms of your hands.

Silence (at least 60 seconds).

Close with the prayer "Come, Holy Spirit." (You might want to keep your paper under your pillow or on your person to help keep focused on God's hand active in the process of this change.)

Or sing "Abba! Father!" or "Glory and Praise to Our God," verse 2.

CONFLICT

CONSIDERATIONS

We all face conflicts—new ones springing or creeping up on us, resurgences of old conflicts never resolved. How do you handle them? Some people get overexcited and upset and cry out to whoever can hear. Some get depressed and crawl deep inside themselves. Others talk it out. Some throw themselves, willy-nilly, into the midst of it. Others avoid or ignore the situation altogether.

What conflicts have you faced in your life? How did you handle them? What conflict are you facing now? How will you handle it?

When conflict confronts you, what do you fear? What do you trust in?

Name one or more conflicts in your life which have turned out to be positive. Was the way you handled it/them positive or negative?

SCRIPTURE

The scriptures give no promises of a conflict-free life, a life on "Easy Street." But they do remind us that through any conflict, any trouble, God will be with us. Read Ps 46 or Is 43:1–2 and silently reflect on the following from Jn 14: "Do not let your hearts be troubled. . . . I will not leave you orphaned." A catechist might share a personal story of going through darkness, through conflict, and witness to Jesus' presence there—or even the struggle to find Jesus there.

The following are examples of conflict in the gospels:

- Mt 14:22–33: Walking on the water;
- Mt 22:15–22: The coin and taxes;
- Mk 4:35–41: Calming of the storm;
- Mk 9:33–37: Dispute about greatness;
- Lk 4:1–13: Temptations in the desert;
- Lk 13:10–17: Healing on the Sabbath;

114

- Lk 15:11–32: The Prodigal Son;
- Jn 18:1–14: Jesus arrested.

Have you ever had an experience of conflict similar to those in the gospels? To which characters in any of the stories do you relate? Which characters do you dislike? Feel sorry for? Admire? Why? Which story confuses you? Why? Do you agree with the manner in which the conflicts in the stories were handled? Has Jesus ever acted or spoken in your life in a similar manner? What conflict in your life keeps you fearful? How might your fear be relieved? Catechists might share personal stories of conflict.

Silently reflect on Is 40:28–31 and Mt 11:28–30. What conflicts in your life weary you? Do you ever look to Jesus to be refreshed? Do you ever give up or act negatively in the midst of conflict? How might you renew your strength or resolve? How do you handle conflicts that just will not go away? Do you ever find rest? How might renewed hope help you? A catechist might share a story which illustrates a response to one or more of these questions.

REFLECTION/ACTION

1. I place before you a choice. A blessing and a curse. Choose life (based on Dt 11:26). When faced with conflict do you *usually* choose life? a blessing? a curse? What does this say about you? Explain.
2. Think of a time in your life when just a person's being there was important. Send that person a card.
3. Has there been a difficult time in your life when the people around you were not "there for you"? How did you handle this disappointment? How did you make your way through the time? Do you think Jesus was present?
4. Have you ever helped a person through a conflict? What happened? Would you do it again? Why?
5. Think of a conflict which has continued to confront you for a very long time. How might Jesus advise you to handle it? Talk it over with someone. Pray about it. Try to do something about it.

PRAYER

All: Sign of the Cross
Group A: I am with you.

Group B: Do not be afraid.
Silence.
All sing a few verses of or listen to "Amazing Grace."
Silence (at least 60 seconds).
Group A: I am with you.
Group B: Do not be afraid.
Group A: I am with you to the ends of the earth.
All: Amen.

FAILURE

CONSIDERATIONS

We fail ourselves.
We fail others.
We fail in important things, in insignificant things.
We rise above failure; we sink under its weight.
We learn and grow by failure and we are stunted by failure.
We can be challenged by failure and we can be devastated by failure.
Failure can scar us. It can open us up. It can point to deep realities—about ourselves and others.
What have you failed at recently? Was it important? How did you feel? Was anyone else involved in one way or another?
How do you *usually* handle failure? What does that say about who you are?
How might others perceive you in your reaction to failure? How do others' perceptions effect you?
Do you know anyone who has never experienced failure?

SCRIPTURE

None of us is perfect. There is only one. It is God. Deep failure can teach us that.
Our failures often hurt us deeply. They are reminders for us that we require tenderness (from others and ourselves), that others, too, must require tenderness and gentleness from us. They help discipline us, keeping our priorities in order, our sense of creatureliness intact, and our yearning for God alive. None of this means, of course, that it is easy. But all of it points to the reality of the God in whom we can find strength, find trust, find forgiveness, find rest.
The gospels offer testimony about failure—for example, the woman caught in adultery in Jn 8:1–11. She finally got caught, "blew it," failed. . . . What about her partner in adultery? What became of

him, do you imagine? What about those who scattered—sheepishly—stones in hand? How might each of the characters have felt? Do you identify with any of the characters? What is the key message? A personal story of failure might be told here.

Read Mk 6:1–6. How do you think Jesus felt about Nazorean response to him? About being unable to work miracles in his hometown? About their lack of faith? Have you ever experienced success "abroad" but failure "at home"? What can failure teach you about yourself? others? How do your failures affect others? How do others' failures affect you? A catechist might relate these questions to a corresponding personal experience of reliance on Jesus' example and help.

Read and reflect on Jn 16:31–33. Do you really believe? Do you ever neglect or reject the teachings of Jesus? If so, how do you handle your failures in this regard? Do you find, amid failures, your peace in Jesus? Do you accept your failures and sufferings? Do you have courage in the face of failure? Do you believe Jesus has overcome the world? A catechist might choose one or two of the questions and relate personal responses.

REFLECTION/ACTION

1. Has there ever been a time in your life when all you had left to turn to was God? What happened?
2. What specifically might God be teaching you through your failures? What message of love is so difficult for you to hear?
3. In the next week, find an hour to be all alone—no music, no book, no TV, etc.—and reflect on God's tender care for you.

PRAYER

Sing or listen to "For You Are My God."
Sit in silence for at least 30 seconds.
A catechist quietly says, "Speak, Lord, your servant is listening."
Sit in silence for at least 60 more seconds.
Pray together "Glory be to the Father. . . ."

BEAUTY

CONSIDERATIONS

A basic experience available to all people on the face of the earth is beauty. Beauty is found all around us. The beauty of nature in particular is an outstanding example—in its most majestic and magnificent as well as in its subtlest or most hidden forms. Each of us experiences beauty in other ways as well—in a baby at the mother's breast, a special sign of affection from a person one loves, a mathematical pattern, a well-executed procedure, or a musical work.

It is often the wonderful gift of beauty that helps to sustain us through our ordinary lives. It can motivate us, quiet us, reassure us, refresh us.

1. What are two examples of beauty you have experienced this month? This week?
2. What beauty do you take for granted? Which do you cherish?
3. Do you ever talk about the beauty you experience? Why or why not? To whom do you or could you speak? Why that person?

SCRIPTURE

Signs of the beauty of God and God's creation are abundant. Read over the stories of creation in Genesis. A parishioner who has a beautiful garden, is a bird watcher, a "museum goer," or a photographer or artist might give a short talk on beauty.

Beauty is universal and is alluded to throughout the scriptures. A catechist might choose a favorite psalm depicting beauty and tell why it is special.

Warnings concerning beauty are also found in the Bible. In Mt 23:27–28, Jesus warns that though the appearance of beauty is present, in reality, inside, there is sometimes hypocrisy or dishonesty or duplicity. A catechist might witness to how she has learned to know what is truly beautiful and what is not.

REFLECTION/ACTION

1. Does the experience of beauty ever awaken in you a spirit of gratitude or thankfulness? Does it ever move you to thank God or
   another person?
2. How can beauty lead you deeply into God's presence and to center
   on what is important?
3. In our society we are often besieged by claims to beauty by adver-
   tisements and a materialistic lifestyle. How might you identify false
   and empty claims to beauty? How might you become more wary?
4. What are the truly beautiful things you experience in life?

PRAYER

Either prepare ahead of time or speak spontaneously a litany of
the beautiful things you are thankful for.
Response: How great you are, O God!
Sing "How Great Thou Art."

Notes on the Contributors

Rev. Ronald J. Lewinski, S.T.L. is a priest of the Archdiocese of Chicago and the director of Chicago's Office for Divine Worship. He is the author of *Welcoming the New Catholic* and *A Guide for Sponsors* published by Liturgy Training Publications. He has offered numerous workshops and addressed many groups on the liturgy and catechumenate in the United States, Canada, Germany and Australia. He was a member of the Bishops' Committee on the Liturgy subcommittee on the RCIA and a charter board member of the North American Forum on the Catechumenate. He serves on the advisory board of the Notre Dame Center for Pastoral Liturgy.

Elizabeth S. Lilly is the Liturgy Coordinator for Saint Thomas Aquinas Parish in Palo Alto, California. She is a member of the catechumenate team in the parish and serves on the catechumenate committee of the Diocese of San Jose. She has contributed to *Breaking Open the Word of God, Cycles A, B, and C,* and *A Catechumen's Lectionary* published by Paulist Press. She has been a team member for workshops sponsored by the North American Forum on the Catechumenate.

Marguerite Main is a Pastoral Associate at St. Louise Parish in Bellevue, Washington. She has worked with the RCIA for 13 years. She is a member of the Steering Committee of the North American Forum on the Catechumenate, and is a team member for Institutes presented by the Forum. She served on the task force in the archdiocese of Seattle to draw up that diocese's first guidelines for the RCIA, and is currently a member of the diocesan RCIA Standing Committee. She is a wife, mother of three, and grandmother of five.

Elizabeth Harubin Sinwell teaches religious studies at Providence College as well as high school religious education. She has taught catechist formation courses, and has been active in the Rhode Island Catechumenate. A frequent workshop presenter throughout the U.S., she holds a masters degree from Boston College.

Joseph P. Sinwell is Diocesan Director of Religious Education and Co-Director of the Catechumenate for the Diocese of Providence. He is a founding member of the North American Forum on the Catechumenate and served on its steering committee. He holds master's degrees in religious education and agency counseling and is a candidate for a doctor of ministry degree at St. Mary's University, Baltimore. Mr. Sinwell is co-editor of *Breaking Open the Word of God,* Cycle A, B and C, and *Ninety Days,* published by Paulist Press.

Barbara H. Zanin is a pastoral associate at Our Lady of the Presentation parish in Lee's Summit, Missouri. Formerly Director of the RCIA for the Diocese of Kansas City/St. Joseph, and staff member of the Center for Pastoral Life and Ministry, she continues to serve as a member of the Institutes Team for the North American Forum on the Catechumenate. She is married and the mother of three children.